God on Our Minds

PATRICK HENRY and THOMAS F. STRANSKY

God on Our Minds

With a Foreword by
Cynthia C. Wedel

A Project of the
Institute for Ecumenical and Cultural Research

1982
Fortress Press   Philadelphia, Pa.
The Liturgical Press   Collegeville, Minn.

Materials previously published in *Occasional Papers* of the Institute for Ecumenical and Cultural Research are used, sometimes in slightly altered form, on the following pages:

No. 1 "Confessing Faith in God Today: A Report," by Patrick Henry and Thomas F. Stransky, December 1976: pp. 5, 14–15, 66, 72, 75–76, 90–91, 134.

No. 3 "Confessing Faith in God Today," by Robert S. Bilheimer, November 1977: pp. 20, 28, 91, 92–93, 96–97, 98, 137, 158.

No. 5 "A Song of Worshiping Pilgrims," by Patrick Henry, March 1978: pp. 11, 12, 15, 32, 46–47, 88–89, 90, 95, 106, 107, 108, 144, 145, 165.

No. 6 "Black Theologians Confess Their Faith in God," by J. Deotis Roberts and Thomas Hoyt, Jr., November 1979: pp. 89–90, 105, 108, 109, 110, 113, 114, 130, 135, 153–54, 154–56.

No. 9 ". . . To Confess Our Faith," November 1978: pp. 84–85, 100–101, 106, 107, 135–36, 144–45.

No. 11 "Further Reflections on Confessing Faith in God," March 1980: pp. 24–25, 26, 55–56, 157.

No. 12 "Why Ecumenical?" by Cynthia C. Wedel, May 1980: pp. 150–51.

Library of Congress Cataloging in Publication Data

Henry, Patrick, 1939–
  God on our minds.

  "A project of the Institute for Ecumenical and Cultural Research."
    1. Christian life—1960–   . 2. Faith. 3. God.
  I. Stransky, Thomas F. II. Institute for Ecumenical and Cultural Research (Collegeville, Minn.) III. Title.
  BV4501.2.H3744   248.2   81–70593
  ISBN 0–8006–1600–6   AACR2

9391K81   Printed in the United States of America   1–1600

In Memoriam
Claire Hahn

"I have learned that I do not have to cringe before God."

Contents

Foreword

I spend my life in meetings and conferences of church groups and various organizations in which I am active. When I was invited to participate in the "Confessing Faith in God" project I agreed because I am a member of the Board of the Institute for Ecumenical and Cultural Research, and I don't like token board members.

I went a little reluctantly. I had seen the list of participants. I had an idea of what it would be like—complex theological discussions using technical jargon which I understand poorly, and arguments over obscure points which mean very little to a lay person struggling to be a Christian. I have been around enough theologians to know that, like any professional group, they nearly always try to "one up" each other by having read the latest book in some foreign language. I didn't expect to take much part in the discussions and just hoped I could look interested and moderately intelligent.

What a surprise awaited me! The first meeting was a brief time of getting acquainted—putting names and faces together. Then we were told to spend the next day alone, writing about our own experiences in relation to God. This was to be strictly autobiographical—no quoting of others, no theorizing, just telling of our own pilgrimage.

Our papers were collected and duplicated; then we met, and each one told her or his story, expanding on what was in the paper. Suddenly these formidable strangers were people—very human, often unsure and weak, sometimes joyous and confident. Many told of long wanderings in disbelief and a slow return to a new relationship with God. Some admitted to being still in the wilderness. No one quoted Tillich, Barth, Küng, or Rahner to score a point. We were speaking for ourselves. I began to understand why it had been called "Confessing Faith in God," for we were indeed "confessing"—speaking out of our own past and present with their high and low points.

We were Roman Catholics, Orthodox, mainline and evangelical Protestants—black and white—men and women. Our journeys had been very different, yet we could feel ourselves living in each one. As we moved through several periods of time together, we all became convinced that one of the great needs of the church and of individual Christians today is to be jolted out of our routine experience of the faith, which so many of us practice with little critical thought, and to be brought back to the basis—God. I thought of the highly educated, competent lay persons I know whose understanding of their faith is still at a fourth-grade Sunday school level. And I thought too of the many ministers and priests who are so caught up in the busyness of congregational and parish life that they find little time for thought or reflection.

My own relationship with God is richer as a result of this experience. I hope that this book will lead others to ask questions and think about their own relationship with God. Read it for a description of the process and as an invitation to join the process, not as a ready-made answer.

I would urge that if you want to experiment with the "confessing" method, you try to gather as diverse a group as you can. It will work, of course, even if you are all of the same age or sex or race or religious affiliation. But it will be far more effective if you are not.

CYNTHIA C. WEDEL

Introduction

Saint Augustine wrote about time: "If no one asks me, I know what it is. If I wish to explain it to one who asks me, I do not know."

Is Christian faith in God like time? We should know what faith in God is; after all, we Christians have at least that in common. Yet if somebody asks us to explain faith, we become tongue-tied, and we break the silence with babble about church membership or creeds or sacraments or being "born again" and having "found it" or moral behavior or the happy face and positive thinking or the discovery of the "real me"—there are dozens of code words and phrases. But sooner or later we catch our breath. Suspicion surfaces: we don't really know. Does our much speaking about faith in God substitute for deep knowing, even cover our doubts?

"Do you Christians really believe what you say you believe?" We can transfer the question into the first person: "Do we really believe what we say we believe?" Indeed, "What does it mean for us Christians to confess an authentic faith in God today?"

In the mid-1970s, the Institute for Ecumenical and Cultural Research began a program of inquiry on "Confessing Faith in God Today," cochaired by the authors. The Institute gathered goodly mixes of people to ask themselves this question in the summer quiet of its facilities on the grounds of St. John's Abbey and University in College-ville, Minnesota. Our group focused on the general ques-

1

tion. Other groups, meeting at other times, were more specific: the meaning of confessing faith in God today as campus ministers and as black men and women. Still other groups in the Institute's program began with other subjects and constantly came back to the question of faith in God: psychiatrists, social scientists, and theologians who explore the human condition, and professional theologians who are concerned with the meaning of sin and salvation in our time. "Confessing faith in God" was faced in steady gatherings of ordinary folk in over twenty-five ordinary Minnesota parishes, Catholic and Protestant.

The fundamental method was expressed, hesitantly at first, by the words "confessing," "confessional," "speaking in the first person." Explains Robert S. Bilheimer, the Institute's Executive Director who gently orchestrated the shared reflections:

> Whatever the phrase, we have insisted that all the participants speak of their own thought, their own conviction, and their own reflection upon what they have learned by study and have experienced in life. This "first person" mode of address contrasts with a merely analytical style in which trends, relationships, and so on are outlined in history or the contemporary scene without commitment on the part of the speaker; and contrasts with expressing opinions, however profound, upon what other people think or should think, without bringing this down to what the speaker honestly thinks for herself or himself. Thus our discussions have insistently brought theology, other disciplines, and life itself together in the person's own grasp and expression of them.

True, the "first person method" can easily be distorted. I can feed a cozy ego trip by turning God into my own shabby image and by eroding all traditional religious authority with a subjective faith.

Yes, but I must first be honest with my own story of faith

in order to allow it to be challenged by the honest accounts of others, and we must be honest together in order to allow our story to be challenged by God's word about all human stories, past and present.

This book records what some Christians have discovered together. Time and again we were surprised, caught off guard, pulled up short by unexpected and unpremeditated insights. The contents of our answers came much more as gift than as planned achievement.

Three summers of preliminary discussion (1976–78) were followed by three summers of intense, sustained inquiry (1979–81). Until the end of the 1980 session we did not have an explicit intention of publishing our in-house materials. The conversationalists had no eye on an audience, no guarded thoughts such as "outsiders are already listening in." The quotations which lace this book are from notes taken of the conversations, from fragments written down, rather hastily, during the solitude sessions of the meetings, from reports of church study groups that asked the question and experimented with the method. The sources of the quotations remain unnamed.

Participants in the three-year sustained inquiry who, in the summer of 1981, reviewed the initial draft of this book prepared by Patrick Henry were the following: Robert S. Bilheimer, Denise Lardner Carmody, John Tully Carmody, Joan Chittister, Donald W. Dayton, Evelyn Durkee, Melvin B. Endy, Jr., Patrick Henry, Thomas Hoyt, Jr., Timothy Kelly, David A. Killian, Janet Huber Lowry, John C. Meagher, Harry A. Nielsen, Don E. Saliers, Thomas F. Stransky, Carl A. Volz, Cynthia C. Wedel. Others who participated one or more times during the six summers of discussion were the following: Constantine N. Dombalis, Peter Ellis, Claire Hahn, Jeremy Hall, Paul Minear, Kieran Nolan, Timothy Power, J. Deotis Roberts, Jack B. Rogers, A. W. Richard Sipe, Mary Jean Schlegel, Archie Smith, Jr.,

Jerome Theisen, David Tracy, Nicholas Triantafilou, William Vos.

The draft was revised extensively in light of suggestions made by the reviewing group, though the authors take responsibility for the final form of the book, including both the selection of texts (from more than one thousand pages of accumulated material) and the interwoven commentary. Thus, what is presented here is neither a consensus document nor the private opinion of the two authors. As a group we found we could say much together without all having to say the same thing.

It will be understood that this book does not represent the Institute for Ecumenical and Cultural Research or speak for it. The authors nevertheless speak for themselves and the group in expressing gratitude to the Board of Directors of the Institute for initiating and supporting the process which has resulted in this publication.

As will be obvious to the reader, we offer here no one-two-three step handbook (though we do suggest). We do not provide a set of answers at the back of the book (though we don't always answer questions with more questions). We attempt, by indirect means, to point to the center of the original task, "What does it mean to confess faith in God today?" We hope to encourage others alone and especially as groups, to venture into that question, always challenging, intimidating, renewing. We hope the reader can say at the end of the book, as each member of the inquiry group could say at our final session, "Now that I am finished, I am beginning."

PATRICK HENRY
THOMAS F. STRANSKY

1
Confessing Faith
In God

"I recently learned that I have terminal cancer." There's a sentence that could stop a conversation dead in its tracks. Instead, the sentence began an extended inquiry into what it means to confess faith in God today. The late Claire Hahn, former nun, Professor of English Literature at Fordham University, barred the door against any abstract, arm's-length speculation. In the face of Claire's openness and her intense engagement with God, any carefully constructed "set piece" about what faith in God means becomes hollow. There can be no role playing, no evading the question: "What, after all, do I know about God, and do I want to confess what I know?"

Claire Hahn's opening statement was not mainly about herself. She went on:

▶ I had encountered such crises at second hand many times in the characters of English literature, but now I was no longer teaching about crisis. I was face up against my own.

In the same hospital room with me was a woman, a black lady who had had both legs amputated. When her bandages were changed, the pain was excruciating and she cried out. The nurse said to her, "Put your faith in the Lord." The woman replied, "When you do that, you get hit," and then asked me, "Do you have faith in the Lord?" "Well, yes," I replied. "So do I," she said, "but do you like

5

the Lord?" "No," I confessed, "I do not like the Lord." "I don't either. God's not our kind of folks." ◀

For most of us, "God's not our kind of folks" is a new way of speaking about God. The statement is uncongenial, even shocking. Nevertheless, it forces the question into the open: "What does it mean to confess faith in God today?" This question focuses attention on the true relationship between Christians and the world. The question is an ecumenical equalizer. It goes beneath particular Catholic, Protestant, and Orthodox identities to the root of Christian identity itself. The question reaches a level of consciousness and conscience at which formal theological learning is not necessarily an asset and may be a liability; a level at which the God who has made foolish the wisdom of the world might gain a hearing; a level at which theology can be reunited with the life of the people of God in the world.

▶ Theology is too important to be left to the theologians. Theologians need to listen to each other, but they also have to heed the people who make, buy, sell, marry, have children, laugh, cry, sometimes feel forced into situations where they are having to do what they don't want to do, long for the freedom to do all the things they would like to do, and who share one thing in common—that the last thing they all will do is die. ◀

Theologians are, of course, people like that too.

True, faith in God is "more a living than a telling," and even faith can be talked to death. "I am now trying to pluck myself, like a Czech dumpling, out of the boiling water. Too much analysis and introspection (How did I do today at this confessing chore?) may break the spell." A merely verbal faith doesn't amount to much. But confessing faith in God requires that we have something to say, especially what we believe God says to us. And there are times when living faithfully is hampered because we do not know how to tell our faith not only to others but also to ourselves. Some of us have "many concepts and little experience," while others have "much experience and few concepts." In both cases, communication and understanding are hard to come by.

Serious, committed lay persons admit bafflement about profound questions.

▶ Most people in our church study group expressed a belief in the existence of a God or "Supreme Power," but there were many questions as to who God is and what God does.

* Is the God of Christianity the same as the gods of other religions?
* Does God direct my actions, or do I act freely?
* Is religion opium for the people?
* Do we make all this up to pacify ourselves?
* Are only Christians going to have eternal life?

We came from different church backgrounds. Most people expressed a faith in a God, but included many doubts. Faith was considered personal by some and hard to define or explain. Some had at one time lost their faith and interest in religion, but are now again "students of Christianity." For most, faith is not a matter of being born again or experiencing a crisis, but it is a process that began in childhood.

Some of us did indicate a significant event or turning point. Some needed to forget logic and reasoning. Others could not eliminate reason. Some talked about acquiring faith, some about realizing what is already in oneself. Some defined faith as accepting Christ; others as being accepted by God. Also, it was said, "Faith is the feeling of the strength of God." ◀

What is authentic faith in God today? This question does not idle on the periphery of our lives. It won't go away, won't leave us alone. "Does the question still stand fresh? Yes, because it is implied in every day's doings and choices." "The question is central to my life. If it gets answered in one way, I am obligated to one way of living; another answer obligates me to something else entirely." Or "What am I to do if, while my uncertainties outnumber my certainties, I long to be loyal and at the same time honest?" We suspect true loyalty to God is not in conflict with honesty to self, but is in fact dependent on it. How do we figure out what such loyalty and honesty are?

There is no shortcut, quick-fix answer to "What does it mean to confess faith in God today?" Confessing faith is not a program or a theory, not a list of numbered declarations or catalogued affirmations; it is not another's prescription for you in a set of "shoulds" or "should nots." The question has to be answered personally, though not alone. When Christians of varying traditions and experiences come together to share their first person reflections on confessing faith in God, discovery takes place. They discover one another, they discover themselves, and they begin to discover God anew.

Does this method make faith entirely subjective? Is turning to personal experience as the starting point one more example of combined excessive introspection and the erosion of all traditional religious authority? Not necessarily. In fact, such a turning may nourish something very different: the conviction that God is really at work in our lives. The turning to experience itself acknowledges the authority of God; and when we explore faith together, we admit that we have a better chance of fooling ourselves when we are alone. Shared discovery that we together have something to say is important today, even though what we say may not be fashionable. So much of our personal and church life shouts an uncritical yes to too much in American culture. American-styled Christianity is losing so many traces of the biblical accent while it is learning the language of political, economic, or military triumphalism ("We're number one!") or of distorted consumerism ("Having more is being more!"). We are cutting ourselves adrift from our moorings in the Bible and church tradition. We are making God into an American kind of folks. As a result, our faith in this congenial, ever-adaptable God provides no vantage point, no stance vis-à-vis a culture which is at one and the same time cocksure and desperate. We run from God's word of judgment and, consequently, are deaf to God's word of true hope and blind to God's ways for us.

For many American Christians, faith has become thin and dim. Some are dissatisfied. They suspect that authentic faith in God is something richer, something tougher, something more starkly and startlingly holy than what we are used to. "We want our confession of faith to have sufficient force so that others will at least say no, and not yawn." "I want to shine with more watts than I shine with now."

2
Pilgrimage

▶ A young couple sits in front of me. Their marriage is a year off, and the question of faith and spiritual life has surfaced. They both believe in God. She comes from a strong religious background. He, on the other hand, comes from a minimal religious background. Some in his family do not believe in God. The problem of evil looms large as he tries to understand a ski accident that has left his brother paralyzed for life. The couple believes in God, but the confession of that belief takes different forms.

A year ago I might have reacted differently—trying to get him to agree with her words and symbols. But an experience last year of several evenings' discussion with members of our parish has taught me that confessing faith in God today is not a matter of easy answers or well-taught formulas. It is much more complex. I listen to him and urge her to listen to him. His struggling experience of God teaches us. ◀

The priest here has three options. One he explicitly rejects. One he does not mention, but many Christians would have taken it: "God is different things to different people, so I had better try to get the conversation onto some other subject." The option he took (the third) is the tough one: if I expect people to listen to my story of engagement with God, I must listen to theirs and be prepared to learn from them. "One-way preaching is not the way to confess faith."

This third option is the way of the Christian who is confessing faith in God, who is searching out what it means to live with God over a lifetime, who wants to see things whole but is suspicious of any premature closure on what the whole might be. For the priest and the young woman, the admission that her fiancé's "struggling experience of God teaches us" marks the beginning of a disciplined search, a life of pilgrimage. Much church life today does not readily identify the Christian way as the way of the pilgrim. A year earlier, the priest said, he probably would have tried to persuade the young man to settle down in the place already fixed by the church.

BEGINNINGS AND JOURNEYS

The Bible does not talk much about fixed places. The Bible is the story of beginnings and journeys more than of endings and settlements. Even the initial Christian community had to learn that Jesus' preaching of the kingdom of God was not the signal for an end to the frustrations of history, but was the beginning of the checkered, often frustrating, history of the church.

Every apparent ending is a new beginning because the initiative is God's. Neither Moses nor Paul received the promises of God in full measure. Both confessed their faith while they were on the way; the very being on the way was their confessing of faith in God. If asked, "What does it mean for you to confess faith in God?" they might well have answered, "Just look where we are, out here in this wilderness, telling what we know, yet traveling along this road."

It can be unsettling to discover that the Christian life is a search, a pilgrimage to God during which we see dimly, as in a mirror. After all, isn't the Christian one who has found it? If faith in God doesn't provide the answers, what use is it?

"Does the pilgrimage work?"

"Maybe it will, maybe it won't."

"Tell me how to make the pilgrimage."

"I can't; you have to join the search."

"Well, if that's what it takes, at least show me your goals."

"The goal is a surprise."

The discovery that we are on pilgrimage can be unsettling; it can also be liberating, even exhilarating.

▶ In our parish, I proposed to the worship committee that a group discuss "confessing faith in God today." The prospect of another program on the church calendar was not so exciting for me, and I half hoped they would say, "It's a great idea, but . . ." I had almost forgotten to mention to them that the key to this program was not going to be creeds, doctrines, experts, or opinions of others. One could only speak in the first person, that is, "My experience of God has been . . ."

To my surprise they jumped at the idea. The thought of exchange in that way excited them. People who had worked together for years found themselves talking on a whole new level of faith (it wasn't just ideas anymore). I surprised myself by realizing how little we allow ourselves or others to share on that level. I wasn't the teacher anymore, but a fellow pilgrim. We grew, we were challenged, we confessed. It was not just another study group—it was church. ◀

It was church because it was a place of discovery. It was no longer "going through the motions," "business as usual," polite formalities designed to keep up conventional appearances. When Christians begin to see themselves as pilgrims, things look different. Personal life takes on a new dynamism. One's connection with tradition—both that which is received from the past and that which is passed on in the present—is clarified. Church itself is subjected to criticism and gets a new lease on life. In all three dimensions—self, tradition, church—the pilgrimage becomes an invitation, not a threat.

PILGRIMAGE AND SELF

Someone who thinks that talk of "pilgrimage" or "search" is the language of halfhearted, thin-souled Christians might well say, "When the stakes are as high as eternal salvation, who can afford to be wrong? How could you say that 'the denial of God may well be a portion of a lifetime's confession of faith in God'? When a church group reports that 'we decided it is all right if our level of trust in God fluctuates from trusting to not trusting,' aren't they simply admitting that their faith in God (if we can call it that) is weak almost to the point of extinction? When someone wonders, 'Will my faith be strong enough if a crisis comes?' isn't the question itself evidence that the faith isn't strong enough?"

To such a challenge there is, in one sense, no reply. Once we assume either that the Bible is an answer sheet to life's exam or that church authority alone has the key by which to read the questions and interpret the answers, we are bound to denounce pilgrims and searchers as unconverted and weak-kneed or willful and proud. Their stories of engagement with God have no use other than as cautionary tales about the dangers of thinking too hard, puzzling too long, and believing not enough.

If the reply is to have any bite, it must question the assumptions. First, when we look to the Bible as part of our history, not as the answer sheet to life's exam, we find it full of accounts of people who thought hard and puzzled long, who had to sweat it out in the wilderness for many long years after their deliverance, who were denounced by Paul for thinking they had already achieved the fullness of Christian life. In the Gospels, the apostles repeatedly misunderstand Jesus' words and actions. The move from a faith which knows no doubts to a faith which struggles with God is not a backsliding or a falling away, but an entry into the biblical world. A faith which struggles is part of growing into the stature of Christ, who prayed that the cup of suffering might pass from him and who even cried out that God had forsaken him.

The second assumption that must be challenged is church authority's sole right to read the questions and interpret the answers of life's exam.

▶ When I got out of seminary, my greatest concern was to do and say all things correctly. It hardly ever occurred to me that the central issue was what faith meant to me. Several years in campus ministry have made that issue insistent, and I have to figure out how to respond to people who have a much larger portion of faith than I have, and to people who admire how much faith I have. The one thing that will no longer do, either for those I serve or for myself, is a mere recitation of the official belief system. ◀

▶ I was ready to leave the convent because I thought a few weak-willed sisters, lacking any real vocation, were changing the whole pattern of religious life to make things easier for themselves; in fact, I saw it not as my leaving religious life, but as religious life leaving me. Then I started studying the social sciences, particularly social psychology, and I realized that my vocation was "to seek God" not in withdrawal or perfectionism but in social communal forms that enable personal growth and obligate a response. Consequently, my life and faith have taken a great turn: to liturgy but not to formalism, to sacrifice but not to masochism. The renewal of religious life has made the religious order a place where I can deal with the problems of credibility and risk that enter my life. My faith has been stripped to the core; easy answers are gone, and when that happens, a person is left nowhere and everywhere, and that is where I am. ◄

Easy answers seldom survive the pilgrim journey; if they do, they are spoken with a different accent. "God loves me" may be a certainty of childhood, but the pilgrim cannot settle in a child's tent. For an adult to say "God loves me" and mean that "God will protect me from sorrow and failure" or "God will keep me happy according to my notions of happiness" is not to confess faith in God. It is to be stuck in an infantile illusion—an illusion which very few children really accept, as we would find out if we listened to them. "God loves me" can be an adult's genuine confession of faith, but it is costly. The woman in the hospital who said she had faith in the Lord, but "when you do that, you get hit," can witness without illusion to the love of God.

Maturity in faith is not a stage one achieves; it is living in a process of reformation through many levels of maturity, and each resting place becomes in turn a new departure point. Maturity is learning how to live in the biblical tension between remembrance and anticipation. The life of

faith is not a matter of having found it; it is, rather,
"growth and deepening in life with one another in the
presence of God. Surely one of the most pernicious distortions of faith is premature closure on understanding who
God is and what is required of us."

There are many appropriate images for the life of pilgrimage: a journey onward and upward, a spiral, an oscil-
lation between contemplation and action. If we conceive
life as pilgrimage, we think and act with both a seriousness
and a lightness of touch that are in short supply these days.
There are urgent challenges aplenty to engage our anger,
our skills, and our energy. But burnout is a danger, and it is
worth hearing that "Christian confessing may at times be
heroic and demand a heroic response, but Christian life, in
my opinion, is not meant to be lived heroically on a daily
basis, so that every day is a nearly overwhelming struggle.
There should be a naturalness about it, a joy, a peace. As
Isaiah says, the word of God is like rain that waters the
earth and always is fruitful. God is patient." "Confessing
faith in God is usually unspectacular." "A genuinely credible Christian life would, I think, make me mysteriously
peaceful and unusually helpful."

PILGRIMAGE AND TRADITION

▶ My grandmother could read and write no language. She
learned to make the sign of the cross from her mother, who
learned it in the back room of her village hut. My grandmother learned to fast, to pray, to worship from her mother
who was taught these truths of life during persecution.
Without this witness I would not be confessing faith in God.
(May they forgive me if my representation is poor.) ◀

▶ Who has had the most influence on my faith? My
mother. She had a vocal faith through much adversity. I

was embarrassed as a child, but I came to realize its value and strengths later when my own children needed help. ◄

► My grandfather lived with us, and I was very close to him. When I was still young, he died. I went to the empty church to sort things out, and our minister talked to me and referred me to a Bible passage. I don't remember what it was, but it helped. ◄

► I used to wonder whether I could really move beyond the love circle of my family; then it hit me that nothing insulates us from the pain/joy of love. This is like a redemptive circle or spiral—if you love you suffer, then you love again at a deeper level, and so on. Somehow the mystery lies in the fact that God is leading us, calling us, and when we become aware of this call, we are compelled to respond—the choice to enter into the mystery is our own. ◄

Stories such as these, more than creeds and official statements, tell us how each generation learns to confess faith in God. The great documents of the church shape the whole context in which these personal "handings on" of the tradition take place; there is no sharp break between the Nicene Creed and, nearly 1,600 years later, the illiterate grandmother's learning to make the sign of the cross. But this grandmother opened the way for her now highly educated grandson to own the historic Christian faith for himself just as, from the other direction, it was the young man from the skeptical family who opened up for his fiancée and the priest the way to own the pilgrimage of faith for themselves. In countless ways, faith in God is always a shared faith.

► The faith that I have began when others cared enough to

share their faith with me. And not only the beginnings; I have also experienced growth in faith by the continued sharing and confessing of others. The knowledge of abiding love has come to me through the confessing of others who have been channels to me of a love that goes beyond their own love. This kind of love has been experienced almost exclusively in the context of not one, but a number of persons living in the unity of the Spirit. Their unity, from which I have known a love beyond the ordinary, invites me into a reality that is stable but not static. My best experience of church is a community of needy people who, by the wonder of reconciliation among them, speak to me of the glory of God and God's presence by inviting me in as I am, loving me as I am, and calling me to a reality beyond my reach if I am alone. ◀

▶ Confessing faith in God is "singing the Lord's song," as I live to become myself with integrity. The song is always at least humming along within me. Sometimes I hum it so low-keyed that only keen ears can sift it from other, foreign tunes that I sing. Sometimes I scream it out so it can be heard amid blaring disharmonies. I try to let the song harmonize with the tunes of others. Sometimes it does, sometimes it doesn't—my fault or their fault, or both guilty, both innocent. In any case, when I get up in the morning, the hum is there and, at worst, the song at least gets me through the day. Yes, it's my song; I freely own it, decide again and again to own it, happily live by it. But I didn't compose the song. God freely gave it to so many others. They have shared it with me. It is our song, my song is. I don't deserve the tune, so I sing it gratefully, even in strange lands. ◀

▶ Most of us have a small repertoire of elders and friends who have largely given us our faith. Knowingly and unknowingly, they have clarified our confusions, evaporated our useless guilts, put up with our stupidities, forgiven our sins. With money or time, their flesh or their talent, they have made our lives bearable, even very good. They are the confessors we all intuitively light candles before. Stretching back through the ages, they become for us the mainline of tradition. In a chain of mutual indebtedness, they encourage us to do as we have been done to, to hand on as we have received, to share with others what they have shared with us. ◄

Few things can warm the Christian heart more than reminiscing about one's private shrine of teachers in the faith. But just as soon as the warmth becomes really comfortable, a chill wind begins to blow, as one church group found out. We value what others have shared with us; we feel awkward about our responsibility to share it with others.

► How important is it to you to express faith verbally to someone else?
 * "It is important to overcome inhibitions. But I admit I seldom do it."
 * "My first reaction was that it's unimportant. But it seems more important now after hearing how others have influenced us. How will my children know what I believe if I don't tell them?"
 * "In this group, yes. In the larger world, actions are more important than words."
 * "I agree with that in principle, but if you live your faith and never speak it, how will people be led to 'glorify your Father who is in heaven'?"
 * "It's really important to talk to people you love and care about. As to others, it's probably important too, even though uncomfortable."

* "My children have to know what I believe by my actions, not by what I say I believe; I don't think I should delve into my children's beliefs."
* "The very idea that we might have a responsibility to share our faith verbally with our children never occurred to us before." ◄

By the things we do and don't do, and by the way we do and don't do things, we are constantly giving off signals. For better or for worse, we are inescapably sharing with others our confessing of faith in God. When we become conscious that much of what we do is for the worse, is there anything we can do other than feel inadequate? One thing we can do is think in new and fresh ways about what the church is, and that begins with realizing that the church is us.

PILGRIMAGE AND CHURCH

"Why is it that my church is the last place I feel I can be myself in expressing exactly what I believe, doubt, or am bewildered by? I do this best, occasionally, after we eight finish our Saturday night bridge."

"In my desperate illness, I lost a sense of community. I had no one I could call 'my people.'"

What hope is there for change? In some places, very little. Where the church is institutionally prosperous, whether the church be conservative, central, or liberal, majority pressure for significant change in its life and structure simply does not occur, or is voiced only in muted accents. But many Christians are restless and dissatisfied. The motives of the restless vary widely, but behind their dissatisfaction there is the perception, frequently wistful, sometimes rebellious, that "church" means something more authentic than what we have.

▶ One day, while I was an undergraduate, I was walking across campus with a remarkable man, the secretary of the Student Christian Association. We were talking about the church, and I said I had no use for it. In reply to his question, "Why not?" I spoke of my church back home to which I had had to go and which had meant very little, and of what seemed to me the general insignificance of churches. "But that is not what I mean by 'church,'" he said. "What do you mean?" "The church," he said, "is the body of Christ, and you are a member of it." I stood still and looked at him; we walked on. I had never thought about that before. ◀

Misunderstanding at this point would be very easy. It's always possible that what presents itself as a prophetic criticism of the church is nothing more than a detached, academic contempt for anything that does not meet one's perfectionist standards. But the challenge to the church to be the church, to be the body of Christ, does not come from sideline spectators. It comes from persons who love the church with a kind of impetuousness, who intend to draw closer for better or for worse, who have given themselves in relationship to the church and to living through that relationship. The quarrels are lovers' quarrels.

The connection between "pilgrimage and self" and "pilgrimage and church" is direct: "As I want the right to discover and grow, the church must be given the right and the time to grow. The only condition is that personal growth is not stifled. With the diminished threat of excommunication, the process is at least more of a possibility."

From one point of view, many churches do allow that sort of personal growth.

▶ My church happens to be one that bides its time. If I

make whatever renewal professions the church asks of adults, it puts no pressure on me to declare that I have experienced even a happy serenity, never mind something extraordinary and once in a lifetime.

"Well now, what's the matter with a church that doesn't even send anybody around to ask me if I'm saved?" If I should work myself into this kind of anxiety, my church would have certain reminders for me: for instance, that it shelters within itself (and even calls "Christian") persons whose being "born again" takes 999 months beyond the first 9; it points to the notion of sin as a condition of human life, which means that even if I say I have renounced everything for Christ, I'm under no obligation to believe myself right off the bat.

This reminds me, then, that confessing faith in God (or anyway in *that* God) doesn't parallel at all the American concept of "making it" or "I've got it made." ◀

From other points of view, however, the church gets in the way of personal growth, and there is a strong temptation to get out of the church in order to get on with being a Christian. To the assertion that "there is no room for isolated Christians, no confession apart from the community of faith," one might reply, "I cannot agree. It is easy to talk about the institutional basis of faith, but faith is interior; it has to do with identity. All people of faith are really heretics at heart." And the question can come, literally, very close to home. "The issue of the personal and communal dimensions of confessing faith comes up in a renewed debate with a husband who wants to be a hermit Christian as far as public worship or church membership goes. I consider the separation of personal and public to be false. If the social sciences have taught us anything, it is the overwhelming social contribution to personal definition. The confession of faith means nothing if totally private."

Members of one church study group admitted to each other: "We are putting less and less value in our own church membership and more value on nurturing Christian virtues in ourselves and others; we feel that there may not be any difference between those within and those without the church, since both groups have really wonderful saints and rotten sinners." Another study group wondered "how to be the confessing church of Jesus Christ and what that means as opposed to just belonging to a church in our time?" Raising this question is a step toward genuine church renewal, but it would be unfortunate if knowing there is a difference between "being the church" and "belonging to a church" led to the easy solution of "un-belonging." Being a Christian means joining a pilgrim people, who are certainly neither limited to nor identical with a church to which one belongs, but the church is the nucleus of the pilgrim band.

If we expect the church to be perfect and find out, as we must, that it isn't, we may lash out at it as having let us down. A certain lightheartedness about the church is healthy. "The sense of common humanity leads me not to expect too much of authority. I believe in it, but my lower expectations mean that I do not have to get up every morning and ask, 'Whom am I going to get mad at today?' Is this cynicism? No. It is a matter-of-factness." "Remembering that the body of Christ possesses both a human and a divine nature, I can laugh at the shortcomings of the human side of the church." "At least half of the church's problem is taking itself too seriously." When we recognize the church's limitations, we may find ourselves called to greater commitment instead of taunting the church with "I told you so!" "In our study group, we found that when we began to accept an imperfect church (because Christ chooses to be limited by the church and by me), we learned to accept the limitations of an institutional church, but without being satisfied with those limits. We accept others, but we are always calling each other to more, as Christ does with us."

Not everything can be swallowed, however. "I do not expect the total Christian life to be manifested in the church. But when that manifestation is *officially* absent, when church authority explicitly refuses to allow it to be present, I am distressed. This is the difficulty now." And to an alarming degree, the problem is lack of imagination. "The Seven Last Words of the church are these: 'We've never done it that way before.'"

▶ In my own life, confessing faith in God today involves putting aside so much of what it used to mean. All the grade school criteria have been tried and found irrelevant: the catechism answers are gone; the idolatrous awe of an omnipotent clergy is gone; the heaping up of private devotions is gone. They are gone in the same way that other idols of society have been brought down to size: the purity of the CIA, the inscrutable genius of the medical profession, and the certainty of the publishing industry, for instance. Some things, in other words, develop a mystique that becomes self-destructive. The trappings of religion, I have come to feel, are like that, and have become an obstacle to faith and an obstacle to the confession of the God whom religion purports to reveal.

When the trappings or cultural structures of religion are put aside, what is left? And if anything is left, can it be sustained?

I believe that much can be sustained. If the old forms cannot be used, they have provided a basis for present growth. Consequently, a confession of faith in God today has come in my life to mean commitment to *presence*, *prophecy*, and *empowerment*.

Confession of the *presence* of God implies coming to a

consciousness of God in every event. It is out of this perspective that the problem of human evil takes on a new
dimension in my life. I come to the conclusion that to use
evil as an argument that God is not God is to argue that only
what makes me feel good is good. Real consciousness of the
presence of God—a derivative of the monastic and con-
templative dimension of my formation—puts in relief the
reality that there is no such thing as a terrible situation, but
that what is terrible is what I fail to let it do to my God-
relationship. What can be terrible is to despair, to destroy,
to demean God's call to find and follow the Exodus event in
this moment.

Rosaries recited in order to buy future security, the for-
feit of conscience to clerical mandate, and the rigid defense
of speculative theology or denominational purity are no
substitutes for this kind of prayerful presence.

Prophecy is the biblical tradition of proclamation. This
need to continue the proclamation of God's justice, of the
equality and dignity of all human life, leads me to question
and confront any structures that oppress whole classes of
people or threaten their development. At one time, my
"confession" would have demanded obedience in the face
of authority—civil, ecclesiastical, social. Now that same
confession demands outrage.

Finally, part of my confession involves the *empowerment*
that grows out of sacrament and community in Christ. To
be Christian without being involved with others for their
sake as well as my own, for my own sake as well as theirs, is
foreign to this later confession.

I believe, too, that it is Christian community that gives
meaning to sacrament. But in this belief there lies for me,
as a woman in the Roman Catholic tradition, the most
difficult dimension of the confession. I am asked to accept a
community that does not accept my kind of people—except
as handmaids—even in its language, let alone its sacra-

mental system. The confession then is one of dogged faith bolstered by weary hope but persistent love. ◀

With the irony that becomes familiar to anyone who gets involved with the biblical God, the outrage of radical confession is rooted in a profound conservatism, "which means to try a central core which has not been really tried."

For centuries Christians have fought over rival definitions of that central core. Some of the issues are far from trivial, but when our chief motive is defense, when energy is expended mainly in countering one another, differences get distorted, blown out of all proportion. If, instead of assuming we know what the central core is ("The central core is what I and my tradition say it is!"), we set about the common task of confessing together a central core that has meaning today, then our differences will appear in clearer perspective. We can learn from each other instead of browbeating, ignoring, or merely tolerating one another. The times call for Christians to try a central core which can only be discovered together.

▶ For confessors, there is not time and resource for petty conflicts. From our mutual strengthening within community, be it local church or ecumenical gathering, we go forward on a journey with God's ragtag army of love. That army does not prize efficiency or the latest technology. Rather, it stops and slows for those who are handicapped for whatever reason, those who are marginalized. That army adjusts its pace to individual differences of all kinds. Its marching music is not martial but lyrical. Our music, the song we have learned from others and must pass on to those after us, will carry us forward in dance step. The goose step, the lock step of oppression, is replaced by the leap and cavort and twirl of freedom. ◀

WHERE DOES RENEWAL
COME FROM?

In moments, usually unplanned and sometimes quite contrary to plan, the church does manage to be "God's ragtag army of love." Is there a chance of its being so more of the time, intentionally? The answer is yes, but with a qualifier. From experience itself we know that God surprises in ways that are not our ways. Often our brand of prudence and wisdom is put to shame by God's imprudence and foolishness. Likewise from experience and sad trial, we know that if we set our minds too keenly only on renewing the church, our renewal plans will slip into our terms, to our greater glory, and the whole enterprise will get eaten up by authoritarianism, factionalism, and masked selfishness. Perhaps the hardest discipline to which faith in God subjects us is the discipline of not being in charge. Of course we beg in prayer for the renewal of the church on God's terms, yet often in the style of Saint Augustine's prayer for chastity—"Please God, renew us and our church, but not yet!"

The likelihood of our fouling things up or at least of our failure is no reason to do nothing. God doesn't ask us to be successful, only faithful. But we can take some precautions.

First, we can try to keep perspective by awareness of the future and the past. "One day I was typing a letter and my finger slipped on the date. Instead of writing '1975,' I wrote '19756.' I was stunned by the limits we set on our thinking. By adding a single digit, I had taken us from the twentieth century to the one hundred ninety-eighth, and the differences between the early church, the Middle Ages, the Reformation, the Enlightenment, and the modern world (which is so often treated as the most decisive new thing in the history of the cosmos) suddenly faded into insignificance. Tradition became set in a larger context."

Second, we can try to be aware of the spread of the church across the world. "Traditionally, churches have believed in the spiritual reality of the church universal and have concretely responded to the universality of their faith through foreign missions. Only recently has there been much awareness in America of the church universal in the modern ecumenical sense: the whole church in the whole world, being members one of another, mission in and to six continents, and mission in partnership. Until this vision of the universal church becomes second nature to us, the reconstruction of church life in the United States will be a reasserted 'business as usual.'"

Third, we can try to keep perspective by alertness to Christian stories different from our own, in the hope of developing a common memory. "Scholars have shown how the common memory of the people of Israel, recorded in the Bible, was the product of worship. The stories of the various tribes were recounted in the presence of all the tribes, and over the generations each tribe came to accept the experiences of the other tribes as its own. In the future, people may make our separate Roman Catholic, Orthodox, and Protestant traditions part of a common memory. We can prepare for that future by weaving those stories together in our own spiritual development."

In creating a common memory, we join forces not only with living Christians not all exactly like us, but also with dead Christians, both those like us and those unlike us. "On the one hand, we are put off by the fact that people of the past inhabited a world very different from ours; isn't it enough of a hassle to try to understand our own time without trying to enter a whole other world? But on the other hand, it can be encouraging to know people who had very different assumptions from our own. Those people may be hard for us to comprehend, but they show it is quite possible to hold assumptions different from ours, and maybe that will help us sit a bit looser to our own. What we think of as universal limits or barriers to faith may be just our own particular hang-ups."

Fourth, we can stop going through the motions of repeating inherited doctrine as if its meaning were always so clear. We can recognize every Christian as a theologian, for theology simply means a "word about God," and every Christian has a word to say about God. This doesn't mean putting inherited doctrine on the trash heap; far from it. Doctrine was developed out of people's confessing of faith in God; it does not set the limits for what faith might be. It is when we build from the ground up that we come to own for ourselves the living power of inherited doctrine.

▶ Creeds have never excited me very much, even though I know intellectually the anguish that lies behind the more famous of them. But last year a group from our church spent some time discussing the meaning of confessing faith in God today. The ground rule was that we could speak only in the first person. In other words, we could not rely on the Augsburg Confession, the Apostles' Creed, or any other list of formulas. We had to formulate our own statements from our own experience (or lack of experience) with God. I do not take creeds lightly or for granted any more. ◀

Fifth, for many Christians who have a lover's quarrel with the church, the hope for renewal lies in small groups with more or less direct connection to the larger church. In some cases, these small groups become the exclusive focus of loyalty, but in a remarkable number of cases people discover "church" in these groups; then they return to the institutional church with a new energy and a new willing-

ness to work for renewal within the system. What is felt
first as a tension between competing loyalties resolves
itself into a new and unexpected loyalty to a new vision of
the church. "From my experience, I believe that the kind of
confessing called for today is the building of Christian
communities. What we need today is not so much a people
who will fight established exploitative institutions as a
people who, while resisting such exploitation, will create
institutions that do serve. Then maybe institutions that are
reformable will re-form for service."

▶ It was extraordinary that two small groups we were in
met regularly with a sense of common commitment to
share a eucharistic liturgy. From that sharing, natural over-
lappings of interest wove further bonds, so that people
shared baby-sitting, made banners together, went to the
city council side by side. It was hard for someone in the
group to be sick without someone else hearing about it. It
was hard for someone with marital or work troubles to feel
completely alone. In our view this was minimal community, but most of the members counted it a prime blessing
in their lives.

An effective Christian community surely would bring
Christians to deeper intimacy than most of our churches
now do. Confessing faith, especially by praying together,
would free us to speak from the heart, to witness to both
the sorrows and the hopes that are in us. We are so closeted
with our emotions that we find any bit of simpatico, any
felt togetherness, an extraordinary event. Faith says we
should hope for much more. ◀

All these steps and others, which have been tried or will
be imagined, carry risk as well as hope. "Every important
commitment is divisive because it steps on toes. The more
radical, the more resisted. Serious confession leads to the

formation of new community, cutting across previous boundaries, and resistance from some of those to whom or with whom we have belonged. Hardly a new story. The balance of daring and prudence cannot be calculated precisely."

Those who have caught this ecumenical vision of a renewed church discover that they cannot ever quite "go home" again. Most of them do not reject the institutional church, but the loyalty to the particular church is a means of expressing the deeper loyalty to that church which is "the body of Christ." For some Christians in our time, "you can't go home again" is not merely a manner of speaking.

▶ The church accused us of heresy and expelled us from our homes with ten days' notice. Those who rallied to our aid and took us into their homes for extended periods were not of our denomination, but Catholic nuns and Jesuits, Masons, Episcopalians, and many others. I discovered that the kingdom of God is much broader than a small sectarian group. I have become more open to the Spirit, much more ecumenical. ◀

When we reconceive our common origins and our common destiny as Christians, not simply as members of this or that particular church, we are "awakened to a strangeness and a power we had presumed already to know." We come to know what it means to "try a central core which has not been really tried." It is not quite right to say we cannot go home again. "We come home—but not to the same room."

3

"God's Not Our Kind
Of Folks"

"God's not our kind of folks." Once we get over the initial shock of such a bold confession, we wonder if these words are awakening us "to a strangeness and a power we had presumed already to know." But then our defenses come up. "Nonsense! The Bible tells us we are made in God's image; Christ is fully human and Christ is God; we wouldn't pray if we couldn't assume God understands us. God is our kind of folks! Surely if there is anything to the Christian message, that's it."

But what "kind of folks" are *we?* Problem-solving, decision-making, conflict-resolving, finalizing, systematizing, prioritizing—the cliché language of our everyday life answers the question we Americans like to ask: "How to?" Sooner or later most of us reach the bottom line and put to everything in our economic, social, and political life the straightforward, practical question: "Does it work?"

"Does it work?" blocks deeper questions. We subject God to the same test. Faith in God becomes one more means of solving problems, making decisions, resolving conflicts, organizing our lives, setting priorities, and finalizing our incomplete and fragile existence. From "how to cope with grief" to "how to lose fat," faith in God becomes the supreme "how to," the yes to the question, "Does it work?"

When we assume that God is our kind of folks, it is so easy to suppose that God will do what we would do—preserve and protect us as we are. Faith in God becomes the way of explaining our good fortune, and we secretly suspect that our good fortune is God's reward for our faith.

▶ Like most people, I would prefer simple answers. I am attracted to a God who is or should be concerned with every moment and movement of our lives on our terms, so that providence seems like a steady protectiveness of our best interests, right down to our financial status. We see this version of gospel on bumper stickers. We are told that the whole duty of the church is to point the way to the One who can solve all the problems of the world.

But such a God is not authentic. My rejection of the notion of God as provider and protector of my every need has its price. I am often deprived of the beautiful concept of practicing the presence of God. I know I won't be bailed out of my foolish errors, nor will I be immune to accidents or natural disasters or diseases any more than anyone else.

As a result, do I lose any sense that God cares about me as an individual? The skies all too easily become empty. The inner life is difficult to cultivate and sustain in the midst of pressing daily affairs of my home, work, family. Community with others is not easily nurtured, given schedules and preoccupations. My being responsible for many areas of life begins to get in the way of building closeness with other people. There doesn't seem to be time or energy or willpower left over.

How can I be accessible to God's will in my present way of life? How does God's otherness free me from self-pity, neurosis, shrunken living? How can a God who is not our kind of folks, while calling me out, also nurture and uphold me in my weakness? How do I keep from pushing God altogether out of my life? ◀

THE DIVINE NO

We Americans are not the only people who want God on our side, who would like divine approval for what is comfortable and convenient for us. And we are not the only folks who have had to learn that God is not so accommodating.

When Joshua was by Jericho, he lifted up his eyes and looked, and behold, a man stood before him with his drawn sword in his hand; and Joshua went to him and said to him, "Are you for us, or for our adversaries?" And he said, "No; but as commander of the army of the Lord I have now come." And Joshua fell on his face to the earth, and worshiped, and said to him, "What does my lord bid his servant?" And the commander of the Lord's army said to Joshua, "Put off your shoes from your feet; for the place where you stand is holy." And Joshua did so (Josh. 5:13–15).

▶ The messenger of the Lord questions our questions and then turns the tables and questions us by a demand for obedience ("Put off your shoes"). God's ways are not our ways or our enemies' ways. Every "today" stands under this judgment. This has never been comfortable doctrine. It was true in Jesus' time too. Luke 13:1–5 reports that Jesus was asked whether people who had recently been executed by the Romans, or some others on whom a tower had fallen, were worse than others. Jesus knew the motive for the question: "If the Master says they were worse, then we who are still alive must be better, closer friends of God." Jesus replied, "I tell you, no. But unless you repent, you will likewise perish."

We in the American churches can too easily say yes to God's being on the American side or yes to a Jesus who makes us such prosperous and happy consumers. What is most alarming about our particular "today" is the faintness with which we hear the divine "No!"

The intellectual and historical problems we have with God of the Bible recede in the face of the moral question. The Bible shows up our sinfulness: our ability to fool ourselves, to think we are doing the good we think we want when we are doing the evil we think we do not want, our ability to smile and smile (the "happy face" has displaced the cross) and yet be villains. To confess faith in God is to throw in our lot with a people who have been called up short by the answer "No!" to the question, "Are you for us or for them?" and who find themselves, not God, under judgment when they recognize that God's not our kind of folks. ◀

We have all sorts of devices for blunting the force of that "No!"

▶ At certain moments we could close our eyes and imagine ourselves in a sculpture studio where gods are being made to order out of clay, playdough, or whatever stuff might be lying around. "That's a nice one, but couldn't we make the arm shorter? Maybe lop off an attribute?" "That one's too big; let's make it so we can walk around it." I'm inclined to say we all do some of this.

We understand in general, too, why we do this. It's part of a long, complex reaction to the fact that something is already in our midst offering itself as a revelation from a God not of our devising; something with voltage enough to make individuals happy indeed or, as can also happen, unhappy for one reason or another. Stabs at redesigning the old God would appear to acknowledge that voltage, but to suggest an unhappy reaction to it.

Various reasons are offered for making a new, improved,

and more suitable target of worship—some cerebral, some visceral, some both. When I fantasize along those lines, for example, it is usually out of fear that the biblical God has in mind to call me in for a complete factory overhaul—to make me more like Christ, one of God's favorites, one of those pampered teacher's pets. Thanks, but no thanks. ◀

FAITH VERSUS "NOT-DOUBTING"

That "complete factory overhaul" we would just as soon avoid is what the Bible describes in various ways: real conversion, incorporation into the body of Christ, enlisted disciples in the forces of the kingdom of God, the "new creation." Those terms are for many of us, however, wet firecrackers—the explosive potential is still there, but they've got to be dried out first. One way to dry them out is to think of a fresh and troubling way of saying the same thing.

▶ When asked my religious convictions, I always put an X in the box marked "Christian" or "Catholic." This, I suppose, tells somebody, possibly a computer, that I am a Christian. But wouldn't the picture be more accurate if they added another box marked, "Standard Life of the Late Christian Era," or better, "Non-doubter"? Does my not doubting that God made human tracks in history amount to faith?

I guess what I want to say is that my not-doubting is a long way from what this Savior-God calls faith. I don't doubt that there was and is a Savior, or that believing in him, having faith in him, is salvation—all of which goes to show what amazing feats of not-doubting I'm good for. But what if my not-doubting is so remote from what God means by faith that, although I doubt not a word of the revelation, neither do I have an iota of faith to confess?

I don't feel I possess at all what Christ calls faith; for instance, where he's quoted in Luke 18:8 as wondering whether he will find any of it on earth the second time around. Christ didn't express any uncertainty about finding the Bible here or the church or a not-doubter like me who even goes to church and annually renews his baptismal vows. But faith—what Christ calls faith—he wonders about that.

Since I evidently do not have what Christ calls faith, and yet it is available for the taking—a gift—then what he calls faith must be something I don't want, something I give the cold shoulder to. This simplifies the search: all I have to do is find something in the Bible that is possible for me, but that in my heart I want no part of.

What we're talking about is exhibited in the Acts of the Apostles. Those agonies the apostles went through were their happiness. Their biggest resource was poverty. For comfort they had floggings. The chains of servitude were their liberty and to rest meant to double the day's load. Weakness was their armor and their prayers were for their enemies. Gut-soreness they called healing. Out on their feet yet goading each other forward to new torments—that was called loving one another. "As Christ had loved," yes, the little rider at the end—"as he had loved."

I want to condense all of this into one sentence: "Lord, forget what I call happy and make me what you call happy." In this plea it is not difficult to see permission granted to God to put me through the meatgrinder feet first or any other way. But this permission is precisely what I can't find it in my heart to give. I don't want to say, "Lord, forget what I call happy." I want God to keep earnestly in mind what I call happy. ◀

"To embrace God is not necessarily exhilarating," and to confess faith in a God who is not necessarily always on our side is not easy. Nor is it made any easier when we recognize we can't control the use God makes of what we do."God really is out ahead of us and is not dependent on what we do for the cause, even though we are called to be fully present to God's will and work." "Confessing faith in God is giving myself 100 percent—like thirsty in a desert is 100 percent thirsty—to God and the biblical revelation of God's purpose, knowing all the while that God may not use the result at all, or may use it in a way I do not expect." "God is present to me in the possibility of my not having to be God myself—of letting go and letting be."

Most of us would acknowledge the biblical claim that power is made perfect in weakness, but that claim runs directly counter to the assumptions of our whole culture, and it is hard for us to admit that God's measures of success and failure are radically different from ours. "The central attribute of God is forgiveness—and it is God's forgiveness, understanding, and mercy that constitute the horrible judgment. God takes people as they are, and in so doing judges us, because we don't take ourselves as we are or others as they are."

WHAT IS "SUCCESS"?

When we reflect on our faith in the God who is not our kind of folks, we slip by habit into judgments such as our kind of folks make all the time. How do we, after all, make our judgments about whether we are living a successful Christian life, whether we are a successful parish or congregation, whether the church as a whole is being successful in our time? For churches that are growing, it is tempting to think that numerical growth of the kingdom of God goes hand in hand with church growth. For churches that are dwindling in membership, it is tempting to remember the tradition of "faithful remnants." For both, the temptation is to indulge in self-justification.

The main reason we resist confessing the God who is not our kind of folks is our fear that such a God demands a thorough transformation of us. To that demand we reply, "Thanks, but no thanks," and thus freely turn down the invitation to discover a genuine but uneasy freedom. There are other reasons for our resistance, too.

▶ It is difficult to express faith in God in words. Words are too inexact, understood in too many ways, to communicate anything as profound and personal as our faith; just as it is impossible to express in words how or why we love another person. We need to find ways in which our every-day lives and actions radiate our faith.

We are limited in our efforts to think or talk about God because God is intensely personal yet totally other than our human experience of persons. I can only express my faith in God in terms of the best I have known or can imagine of love, understanding, compassion, aspiration, humor, de-light raised to the highest degree and combined with total and absolute power.

I believe that God created us human beings "in God's own image" because God wanted love in the universe; and to create love, God had to create beings capable of a loving relationship with the Creator. Real love must always be an absolutely free gift. We could have been created with an inborn instinct to love God. But this would have re-moved our freedom of choice and the reality of our love. God had to take the risk of creating beings who were truly free (unlike anything else in creation, so far as we know), who could refuse to obey, who could go their own way, who could even deny the existence of their Creator. Then God set about the task of wooing and winning the love of the creature. ◄

GOD'S DARING

The God who takes risks is not a comfortable companion. From such a God surprises are likely to come, and while we may say we like surprises, our general behavior gives a different impression. We insure ourselves against sudden unfortunate occurrences, we consult horoscopes and economic forecasts, and millions of us read the Bible as though it contained a play-by-play prediction of what is happening and will happen in our time.

Just how far does God's daring go and what does God's daring mean for a confession of faith? Some Christians would go further than others and say that an authentic response to the daring God of the Bible carries us to a point from which many elements of the biblical portrayal of God must be criticized.

▶ Authentic confession is confession of what is true and real, what is valuable. When we aren't in a position to discern the truth, then we must confess what rings most true and gives most reality, what establishes most value. The various pictures of God—almost the various Gods—of Bible and church give us a good start if we remember that they offer only hints toward our own responsibility in forming a confession. Confessing them is a form of play, limbering us up for the confession that is not play.

I sing in worship to arouse an appropriate joy or sorrow. In a similar way, I can confess the God of the Exodus in order to awaken appropriate attitudes; the God I must truly, unplayfully confess has something of this faithful caring, something of this saving graciousness, and ought to be accorded the sort of admiration and gratitude the story stimulates. But the God of true confession must be protected from most of the attitudes that arise in me in response to the biblical portrayal of God's dealings with the Egyptians at the time of the Exodus. The hint is partial and clouded.

Bible and church keep trying to tell me that it isn't play; I must respect this, but stay playful all the same. All the Gods are helpful if I stay playful about them; otherwise, my confession loses authenticity. When I find something limp or clouded or incomplete in my confession of faith, I must find a way to play that will help correct it. Bible and church offer wonderful resources, but they are incomplete. I must find other Gods to play: God the Mother, God the Dancer, God the Laugher. ◄

The Bible and church speak in many different ways. While some Christians consider this notion of a playful reading of Scripture well beyond the boundaries of anything that could claim traditional authority, there is much support in Christian history, and even in the Bible itself, for such moves beyond the literal sense of the biblical words. Theologians have talked about how the Bible hides God as much as it reveals God; interpreters have sought meanings at many levels besides the literal; and in John 16:13 Christ himself promises to send the Spirit who will lead his followers into all the truth.

There is an abiding danger, of course, that authentic following of the Spirit's leading will give way to "anything goes." That danger could drive us to give in to the equally serious threat, straitjacketing God in rigid categories. If that happens, we do not simply make God into our kind of folks; we make God our prisoner—though God cannot be locked up for long. "Every time I have tried to put God into a box, God has hit me from another side, an unexpected new area or idea."

KEEPING CONTROL

Our desire to keep God under control illustrates how devious we are. When we are in our "take charge, go get 'em" frame of mind, and don't really sense that we need God's help because we are in control, we are happy enough to think of God as sovereign and free, as our kind of folks. But we have another frame of mind in which we feel utterly powerless in the face of social, political, and economic forces that bear down on us from every direction. When we are thus out of control and know we need God's help, we become uneasy at the thought that God might really be so different from our kind of folks as to be free and spontaneous. What we find so hard to comprehend is that God's freedom is both the origin and the boundary of our own freedom.

▶ If we would confess a God who has acted and is present to us, we surely must first of all be people who take charge of our lives, recognizing where we are manipulated and where we are sedated. Our creations have taken control of their creators. The result for many is a deep sense of personal insignificance, because persons who employ their creative faculties in few or no areas of their lives lose their self-respect, personal power, and sense of being alive.

With no control over important areas of our lives, we lose our sense of any say in our destiny, we feel that we are only cogs in the machinery we have created. The machinery now seems to follow irresistibly its own laws toward the destruction of its own creators. If we can regain faith in our own creative powers grounded in the Creator of our being, then we need not be overwhelmed by the creations of humankind. ◀

In other words, we can say that God is our kind of folks—but only when we recognize in that declaration a judgment on ourselves, not a message of congratulations to God. "God is our kind of folks when we become purified enough to want nothing but God's will."

CONFESSING

And that is the whole point: we answer the question whether God is or is not our kind of folks by the way we confess our faith.

▶ "Confessing" is not an easy concept to grasp, but we can agree on some features of it. Confession means more than making intellectual statements. Confession is a communication which reveals some of the depths of our inner feelings and motivations. If we have experienced or grasped something of God's action or purpose, our confessing of this can be a channel through which God may touch another person.

Confession need not always be verbal. It can be an act of loving acceptance or simple service or courageous standing up for the truth. It can sometimes be just being with another person in a time of crisis or difficulty (or joy!). Acknowledging our own weaknesses, failures, or sins—in the traditional sense of confession—may at times be wonderfully helpful to someone who is struggling with problems. Such confession is possible only when there is some hope of understanding and forgiveness. In most people's experience, the supply of understanding and forgiveness is scanty! ◀

We confess our faith in countless acts; our faith is also shown in the way we do all the things we do.

▶ The world—including myself, others, relationships (racial, national, universal, sexual, class, church), and all other catalogued destinies—I experience as a shifting, surprising theater of loves and hates and lusts and indifferences and manipulative power plays, of inhuman cruelties and superhuman carings, of ecstasies and vomitings, of extraordinary ordinary ways.

But this world I also experience as not being alone. It is all-embraced by a God who loves and whose haunting, judging, forgiving presence demands full liberation in every area of human existence. This fact and mystery of God is heightened in Jesus of Nazareth—God freely human like us in all things but sin (that is, the One who freely is not destructive).

Thus, I experience reality as ultimately friendly. This experience I choose to accept, while at the same time not regarding it as coming initially or sustainingly only from myself. But I do not understand this fact, except to know that to ignore the fact is freely to place myself in a meaningless hell (as Dostoevsky said, hell has no meaning because it is a place where there is no love).

Every other "smaller" fact I take a chance on in the interpretation of any or all human events, including my own life (and including what goes on in the church, that community of those who explicitly believe in, submit to, and occasionally argue with, such a God—not of our own devising, surely).

I am not surprised to find in many a lack of faith or a distorted faith or a shaky or overconfident faith or even a couldn't-care-less nonfaith. But I continue to be surprised at the authentic quality of faithfulness in so many; for the most part, they live a life of such confessing without too much conceptualization or introspection. I appreciate more and more the inexplicable grace of faith: we love God because God first loves us. ◄

To say that reality is neither hostile nor indifferent but ultimately friendly can mean many things, and some of them completely out of tune with the authentic biblical understanding of God. If we mean that God will smilingly maintain the status quo in which we are doing quite nicely, thank you; if we mean that the fate of the kingdom of God depends on America's being number one in the world, so God is under obligation to be at least a little more friendly to our nation; if we mean that when we hear Jesus denouncing the Pharisees as hypocrites, we think he is talking about somebody besides us—in all these cases, we blaspheme God. We have not understood that the friendliness of reality is a call to repentance, to being born again and again and again throughout our life. God's presence is haunting, judging, and forgiving, and it is all of these all the time. We simply cannot slip the living God into our purse or pocket.

► In confessing God my own focus is the event or gift of the life, death, and resurrection (life in death and death in life) of Jesus Christ as presenting anew the mystery of the One who comes, who suffers, love who is God, and thereby the final trustworthiness of reality. The challenge remains a scandal or mystery to me: that, in spite of all, the final word about reality is love, and the final attitude needed to transform our self-centeredness is trust in that reality of God. ◄

Even when we recognize God's love within a full awareness of the range of carings and cruelties, vomitings and ecstasies, so that without rose-tinting our spectacles we can see and say that it is God's world and God is good, our confession of faith may be thin because we assume faith in God is a private matter. "We are reluctant to verbalize our faith because we have been raised in a culture which warned us to avoid discussing politics and religion." That same culture is now full of talk about both subjects, but talk which is often strident and accompanied by very little careful listening.

▶ God's otherness is most clearly the message in community. There in community, with the diversity, disagreement, dedication, and devotion, we connect with the variety of human life and recognize the Creator as beyond our puny imaginations. Yes, it fascinates me that the good and the bad of community life can convey God's otherness. Both can point the way, but only together do they give some clue to the God who is all-knowing but never to be all-known.

Many who have experienced a more personal relation with the Creator than I have would disagree with this location of otherness in community. But for me, community is so much the source of the relation I have with God that privatism is impossible, and moments of inspiration, even secluded ones, tie me more closely and intimately to others. ◀

COMMUNITY AND WORSHIP

The covenant community—those whom God has called and who have covenanted or bound with each other to make their confession of faith together—is the place where God is best known.

The Bible is not, after all, mainly about individuals. God deals more with peoples than with separate individuals.

Worship is, above all, a *people's* confession of faith in God. "When I think of my experience of God, which I tremble to do, and of confessing faith in God, I come to the point where I cannot cogitate anymore, but rather kneel down. This comes through the community of the faithful—the words come after the experience. It happens."

Many persons today insist that worship is properly an individual activity (communing alone with nature, privately reading the Bible, silently praying during the working day). There is undoubtedly much value in private devotions as part of a disciplined spiritual life; there may even be times when the only way to maintain one's spiritual sanity is to take a route that leads away from association with others ("I had to get out of my church in order to preserve my faith"). But over the long haul and by itself, private devotion is not an adequate confession of faith in God. "The Christian fact is not a teaching, but people —the Trinity, family, persons in need, friends, even enemies"—and the people worship. "Baptism, Eucharist, confirmation, marriage, sickness, and death link the confession of faith in God to critical life moments. For me, the joys of human life are heightened in celebrations of worship, sorrows are made bearable by the comfort of corporate prayer."

▶ Confessing faith is, first of all, to praise God. This is our chief end. We give glory to God prompted not by possible rewards, but by love and wonder. This is a countercultural activity, contrary to societal values today. Liturgy is a great help in giving praise. Confessing of sin, prayer, the Eucharist, vestments, absolution, mutual love, resurrection joy—all are powerful reminders that we are not "of the world." Although the praise of God can be done privately, in its corporate exercise it has most potential for a confession of faith to the world, as is shown by the attempts of totalitarian regimes to suppress the seemingly innocuous "doing" of the liturgy. ◄

► True worship does not confuse God with the world. Gratitude, trust, and obedience are not simply the result of being well-adjusted or well-placed in life. Confessing faith requires a critique of culture precisely because the God who is worshiped can never be fully identified with what is known in the world, much less with the accumulation of all the cultural values that make up systems of religion. ◄

GOD AND OUR KIND
OF FOLKS

God's not our kind of folks. For just that reason we can begin to learn what God truly means for folks like us. In the community of God's people and in the act of worship we learn of sin and hope; we learn to live within the tension between "the world as we experience it and the world as God declares it and wills it to be." We learn that the ultimate ground for our hope lies precisely in the divine "No!" to our self-interested query, "Are you for us or for them?"

► Do we have to suppose that confessing faith in God is some one thing, interior or exterior, that all Christians do, or all serious Christians do? I'm inclined to think of it as an understanding that goes along with everything we do, the most diverse things—work, rest, worship, suffering, amusement, and so forth—the understanding that God is in charge and is mindful of what we do.

What about the present scene? Churches complain of a haze over that understanding, near failure of communication with congregations and with many young people, a falling barometer of hope, terrible storm warnings, increasing waves of trouble for the poor, the old, minorities, and war clouds. On the scene are many people without hope. They doubt whether there will be a future for themselves or maybe for anyone at all. They want to believe God is in charge but just can't.

What have we got that might be injected into this larger scene (whether our injection takes or not)? For one thing, we have hope and are able to say why we have it and why we never run out of it. Likewise, we recognize grinning, muscular, all-but-unstoppable evils, but we don't see them as necessarily winning, and we can give reasons for this. Likewise, we haven't given up on the future for this nation or the world or the human race or anyone in particular.

As Christians, we maintain that our grounds for hoping all things, holding on and not giving up on the future, go back to a common understanding that crosses denominational lines. That is, the totally unexpected happened in history—the scandal of the cross, Christ risen from the dead, the foolishness of God—on account of which there are such people as Christians. In view of the totally unexpected having happened, every finite hope gets a new lease; nobody can say for sure what couldn't still happen, and everything earthly comes under a freshened perspective.

By that I'm suggesting: the totally unexpected tells each of us in a quite personal way, "Listen, the worst thing that could happen to you has nothing to do with industrial pollution, the class struggle, Three Mile Island, corporate crime, and so forth. You can't very well ignore these things, but . . . ." Also: "Listen, the most important thing about you is not your race, sex, freedom, draft status, and so forth. You can't very well ignore these things, but . . . ."

To many people young and not so young, this word comes as a shock wave of the totally unexpected, if not immediately as a revelation. Hope, courage, perspective, and community (in whatever order) flow from the revelation. Is this not the thing we ecumenically attest to and rejoice in across church lines? Isn't this what we mean to inject (results unpredictable) into the choked and choking atmosphere? ◀

▶ So we tell people: Because God's not our kind of folks, things can be well. God can answer, there need be no dead ends; it can happen: hunger appeased, fear allayed, justice done. Why can we say this? Because God has answered, has broken dead ends, fed desperate spirits, calmed the storms of fear. God has made near those who were far, has made a constantly new beginning. That God has done all this for us and for our salvation is the most important thing about us, much more significant than our status or circumstances. Unleashed with soft voices and knowing hands, this message is the one thing necessary, and we have it to confess. ◀

4
The Fine Line

"The one thing necessary" immediately raises questions about the Christ who claims in John's Gospel, "I am the way, and the truth, and the life; no one comes to the Father, but by me" (John 14:6).

▶ The uniqueness of Christ: this is the one claim that stops me. Because I believe both that Christ is indeed unique and that God is revealed in other ways, just as powerfully and just as "effective to salvation." But what if a Christian becomes a Buddhist? Even my second-grade teacher would have given room for "God's mercy." ("Sister, what happens if some people leave the church and go to another church? Are they saved?" Answer: "It depends. If they really didn't know they were leaving the one true church, God will certainly forgive them.") But is it only condescending mercy, a slip that will be quietly forgiven provided there's no stampede? Or if there is a stampede, will we be forgiven because we've been misled? Or is God the goal and Christ only a way? Or the Way? But that takes us back to the question, doesn't it? ◀

There is a fine line between putting Jesus into the category of eminent religious leaders and championing him as the one path to salvation. Is it possible today to remain poised on that fine line?

▶ Are we supposed to believe, in the face of all the goodness in the world, that we're the only ones who know and serve the real God? That the Bible is God's only revelation? Or do we all know a different side of the same God? Or the same side of the same God through a different source? And what about Christ? ◄

This issue troubles Christians today. The questions are pointed and sharp and probe deeply into the authenticity and authority with which faith in God is confessed. "The question of continuity, of what is always true of Christians in the church, is the key. The central point, of course, is that Christians have always believed that Jesus Christ is God." "Knowing Jesus is knowing God, because they are the same." "If Christians fail to insist that Jesus is the unique Son of God, they have given the game away. There is nothing left of the Christian faith to confess." "The only uniqueness possessed by the Christian church in contrast to other religions is the worship of Jesus Christ as Lord. I define a Christian as one who worships Jesus as Lord." "It is becoming clearer to me that I, at least, can confess faith in God only through Christ. In part, this is rooted in a growing fascination with the concept of the lordship of Christ as a key issue and organizing principle."

CONFESSION AND PUZZLEMENT

For many, however, precisely these claims about the identity and centrality of Christ make the problem. "I find that the heart of my confession of faith is also the nub of my puzzlement." Study groups in three different churches could not avoid the issue.

► Jim said that Jesus Christ is for him the practical working model of what God is like: healer, teacher, philosopher, leader, friend. "He is the part of God that I can understand." Gretchen believed that Jesus is the direct link to understanding God, whereas there are flashes of insight all around us. Charles felt that there is God with or without any Jesus Christ; Jesus is an extra blessing. Jim said that the unique thing learned from Jesus, which is not in all religions, is love. Gretchen was convinced that Jesus made the difference in her wanting to do something about her religion, something with love. We also talked of the psychological dimensions of what it means to be loved, and then being set free to love others. ◄

► Most people in our church study group saw Jesus as a model, leader, teacher, or prophet. Some had difficulties with his human aspect, others with his being the Son of God. Some saw Jesus as Savior; others, as a pivot in history or as an example of spiritual leadership. The importance of the cross and resurrection was clear to some; others wondered about the difference between Jesus' resurrection and other resurrections, such as that of Lazarus. There were questions about interpreting the miracles. Also: "Is it possible to be a Christian without believing in Christ?" ◄

► In our discussion group all agreed that Jesus Christ is "one of the ways to God." "No one comes to the Father, but by me" was rejected. "All peoples have a Christ figure. We don't have a lock on him." "As Christians, we don't have it made, but we have a responsibility." "Christ is a representative type. Others can be Christlike in a given moment." "Christ embodies what we can strive for. I can identify with Christ, not with 'ethereal God.' Jesus was tempted as we are." More traditionally, "Christ is the fulfillment of all, the living symbol of God." At no time did anyone say "Jesus is God." ◄

In light of this variety and even confusion about the role
of Christ in a confession of faith in God today, some suggest avoiding the discussion altogether.

▶ I am inclined to urge that we deal as little with the place
of Jesus in the scheme of things as we possibly can. Anything we might say would be too much for some and too
little for others; no amount of refinement would be likely to
alter that. We must of course affirm that our confessing is
deeply conditioned by our relationship to Jesus, but such
things can be said without getting into uniqueness and
exclusiveness issues.

The confession of God includes an affirmation that we
confess the God whom Jesus confessed as Father. I do not
think that we need to, or that we should, deal with confessing Jesus, so I do not see the need for taking a stand about
his uniqueness, universality, indispensability. My own
position is skeptical (I don't think there are good grounds
for the more dramatic claims made about the person and
work of Jesus) but grateful (I do think much of what seems
to me best in Christianity comes from Jesus' teaching and
work), and if I am altogether unsure about how far we can
go in making claims about Jesus, I am equally unsure that it
is important to do so in any of the traditional ways.

Most of what I hear about the place of Jesus in confessing
God reminds me of what I used to hear about the place of
Mary in confessing Jesus. Both remind me of patriotism:
appropriately pious, tending to promote and consolidate
worthy values, thoughts, attitudes, behavior—but readily
subject to ideological abuse. We tend to lose sight of what
is optional and of what is distorting. I admire gratitude and
loyalty but I think confessing God puts everything else into
a state of question, provisional and tentative. And we
should remember: not affirming Christ's uniqueness is not
the same thing as ducking it. ◀

How can people who are serious about their Christian faith disagree so sharply on the place of Christ in confessing faith in God? The question, "Is it possible to be a Christian without believing in Christ?" may appear absurd, even blasphemous. But the question arises from within Christian confessing itself, not from "outside agitators." The issue cuts too close to the bone to be left unaddressed, even though what we say may be "too much for some and too little for others."

At one level, ecumenical discussion forces the issue. In a gathering of lay persons "the Catholics spoke of the emphasis they had grown up with which stressed the divinity of Christ almost to the negation of his humanity. The Protestants agreed that they had started with Jesus' humanity and had come to recognize the mystery which is his divinity. So we had come together in our confession."

CHRIST AND THE
GLOBAL VILLAGE

The ecumenical discovery of other Christian traditions may loosen us up to consider dimensions of the Christ question that have remained unfamiliar to us in our isolation from one another. But our whole cultural situation, our life in a world intricately linked by all sorts of communication, gives such inescapable urgency to the place of Christ in our confession of faith in God.

▶ Our intellectual situation in the global village causes confusion. We are sharers of a faith which has spread to all areas of the world, which has claimed that Christ is the one true way and his particular act of salvation is the prerequisite of all salvation everywhere and in everyone.

At the same time, we are presented with a world situation in which the claims and strengths of other than Chris-

tian faiths are made known to us in a new way, in which
Christianity doesn't seem the wave of the future, and in
which the conditioned and relative nature of all truth is
pressed home. Is this situation simply a new version of the
"scandal" of the gospel? If we fail to press Christian truth
claims and cosmic views of Christ, can we still remain in
enough continuity with the tradition to be called Christian? How do we handle the fact that on the intellectual
level the various religions are apparently giving very
different, if not opposing, views of human nature and
destiny?

Our confession of faith must be set in the context of the
twentieth-century global village. While avoiding the rel-
ativism that says any view is as good as any other, we must
make clear the universality of God's presence and activity,
our openness to radical transformation of our intellectual
framework through the dialogue between religions, and
our recognition of the relative novelty of this posture for
Christians. ◄

The question of Christ is especially hard for Christians to
deal with because it is not just an intellectual problem. In
the global village, Christians have an uneasy conscience
about traditional Christian claims—and the conscience is
uneasy because we seem to be in a no win situation. It
seems we must choose either to be unfaithful to the Christian heritage or to treat those who are not Christians in a
condescending way. "There is a modesty required of all
who would pour God's absoluteness into the human reality of Jesus Christ—on all who would propose a 'high'
doctrine of Christ. Nonetheless, I doubt that a 'low' doctrine of Christ is faithful to the orthodox tradition, so I am
willing to risk abuses of Christ's uniqueness in order to
keep faith with what past believers have confessed." "I
prefer to break with what past believers have confessed

rather than to stress a uniqueness that can at best make non-Christians 'anonymous' or 'crypto-Christians.'" "Must we break with some categories we have been given in order to prepare for the future?" Even if some of the cherished categories can be retained in good conscience, we must remember that "although Christ is our Savior whose life, death, and resurrection have radically transformed human life and who in some sense died for the sins of the world, we must allow great latitude here and search for more light."

An uneasy conscience can make us uncomfortable, also ineffective. The gospel imperative to be God's messenger to the world is undercut by the haunting suspicion that the world may know as much or more about God than the church does. "Can one believe God is revealed in other religions and still conscientiously be helped by and minister through one's own?"

Christianity and other religions can be dealt with at length in all sorts of theoretical ways that avoid direct, personal engagement with the question. And the theoretical discussion itself takes on a new liveliness when it is prefaced with the personal challenge: "What does it mean to say that Christ had to die in order for Hindus to love their neighbors?"

▶ The central conviction in the confession of Christianity through its entire history has been that in Christ, God saved the world. Now, just as no two people or historical figures are identical, so Christ as a man and as a Savior is unique. I do not necessarily have problems either with the claim that he provides unique insights into the nature of God and (or because) he is uniquely divine. The issue for me is whether he is to be seen as the causal agent of all salvation—the Savior of the world who makes possible all salvation. I'm not sure I know what that means, but when I read documents making that claim or talk to people who make it, I find a disturbing literalism in the understanding of God's relation with creation—even if no clear explanation is given why Christ had to die and rise again for the world to be in a state of potential salvation.

Even if I knew what it meant to tell a Buddhist that Christ died for his sins or made her salvation possible, I wouldn't make that claim for the same reason that I wouldn't tell a woman she couldn't enter the kingdom of God (or be a minister or a priest) unless she were to be viewed as an "anonymous male" on the grounds that Christ was male, no matter how much Scripture and tradition support this claim. ◄

CONTINUITY WITH THE PAST

The general question of Christianity and other religions is made concrete by asking, "What, after all, do I really think is the spiritual state of my Zen Buddhist daughter, or my Jewish son-in-law, or my Hare Krishna fellow employee?" The related question, "Can Christianity respect the autonomy of other religions and still maintain continuity with its own past?" can be focused on the Bible and on the use Christians have made of Christ.

▶ The Bible affirms that humankind, through sin, had become separated from God and was consequently in a state of damnation and unable to achieve the destiny for which it had been created. Christ, through his life, death, and resurrection, reconciled God and humankind, and gives humankind in general and all human beings in particular the possibility of achieving their destiny.

My problem is that this central confession implies something I find incredible.

Acts 4:12: "And there is salvation in no one else, for there is no other name under heaven given among men by which we must be saved." This appears to say that Christianity is the one true religion, the one true way of salvation for all people, and Christ is the Savior of all who achieve their destiny.

1. To say that Christianity is the one true religion implies that others, though they may incorporate true insights into the human condition, are essentially false: they lack the answers. Christianity is the only universal religion to make this claim. The others say: we find meaning here—try it, or there are many paths, or ours is relatively better for people further along the way. Only Christianity says: ours is the one true way.

2. Christ is the Savior of all who will be saved. This used to mean, "Outside the church, no salvation." Now it means, "God can save whom God will as a result of their use of the knowledge God gives them, but since they don't recognize Christ their Savior, they are saved in spite of themselves." I find this claim unacceptable. The biblical portrayal of the human condition—sinful and in need of divine power for renewal—I find meaningful; but in the day of one world, I can't believe that only in Christ does one find true knowledge of God and fulfillment of one's destiny. God's ways may not be mine, but if I am in the image of God, God's conception of justice can't be all that different from mine. ◄

► I find no embarrassment in confessing the uniqueness of Jesus Christ, the Lord of all, indeed the one in whose name all are saved. But I am embarrassed by what we Christians have so often done as counterwitnesses to the

Lord, "the faithful and true witness": committing acts of spiritual violence (using Jesus as a club to herd people away from damnation), being intolerant of others ("You are nothing in God's eyes or God's heart unless you explicitly believe in Jesus Christ as Lord and Savior"), justifying what were in the past blunt but are at present more subtle imperialisms (the rights of God-squads prevail over mere human rights, including the right to be free from the manipulative hard sell). After all, we Westerners consider ourselves political, economic, military, and social superiors to the rest of the world, so why not religious superiors as well?

In other words, I do not question Peter's confession of faith in God: there is salvation in no one else but Jesus. But I rebel against the conclusions some have drawn from that confession in their own evangelistic attitudes and motivations, doctrines and practices. At least I should remember that my commitment to the Lord is also a commitment to the one who came to serve; in fact, I am called to be a "slave of all." Jesus became Lord by emptying himself, not by controlling or possessing others for his own glory.

Jesus the servant strove to fulfill God's dream of a mended creation, the kingdom of God, not to execute a plan for a "Christianized world." The dream remains a mystery; that is, exactly how God does the mending beyond Christian frontiers, how God's saving favors are lavished in and through others who bear not the name of Jesus. As a servant of Jesus and to others, I am called to confess his name by the humble witness I give to him by mending the world's hurts. I rejoice with whatever success God has with those mending ones who do not confess the name, just as I praise the same God who, through us, draws others "from all nations" into explicit discipleship "in the name of the Father and of the Son and of the Holy Spirit." ◀

BEYOND THE IMPASSE

The "central confession implies something I find incredible"; "I do not question Peter's confession." Is there a way out of this impasse? If we insist on posing the question in an either-or fashion—either we remain faithful to the tradition or we remain open to our non-Christian friends—there probably is no way out. However, if we abandon the effort to work out a theoretical solution and begin reflecting on what is really involved in confessing faith in God through Christ, we might discover unexpected resources for renewed energy and effectiveness. Christ will still be part of the problem—he always will be—but in the confessing of our faith as distinct from theorizing about it, he may become part of the solution.

"My doctrine of Christ is exclusive; Jesus is inclusive." "Christology begins with our questions about Jesus, but ends with his question to us, the same as to Peter in John 21:15: 'Do you love me?'"

▶ To me, Christ *is* God. Not all of God, but God's decision to become incarnate in the hope that we human beings might be able to grasp something of God's nature if we could see at least as much of it as could be contained in a human person. While on earth in human form, God was also still "out there" in transcendent completeness—and it was to God that Christ prayed. It doesn't fit any human logic, but God is not bound by human limitations—no problem for God to be in two or more places at once.

But I suppose I puzzle about the fact that, while for me the revelation of God in Jesus is complete, I cannot be sure that God is not self-revealed in Mohammed, the Buddha, and others. I find Christ the final and perfect revelation, but God is the only one who knows the place of the other great religious figures. ◀

In other words, when faith is being confessed, Christ can take care of his own prerogatives; he does not need us to blow the trumpet on his behalf. The Christian's embarrassment at exclusivism in Acts 4:12 can be lessened noticeably by remembering Mark 10:17–18: "And as he was setting out on his journey, a man ran up and knelt before him, and asked him, 'Good Teacher, what must I do to inherit eternal life?' And Jesus said to him, 'Why do you call me good? No one is good but God alone.'"

▶ God has left traces everywhere; those led by the Spirit care little for names. A confession of Jesus' divinity expresses a faith that intends God. Jesus can remain limited, fully historical, less useful than other great seers for certain problems. Plato can say more about politics, the Buddha more about enlightenment. But Jesus remains the exemplar of saving love, which Christianity finds the nearest index of God's essence. ◀

▶ Our knowledge of God is through God's self-disclosure: in nature through creation, through the Scriptures, and in Jesus Christ, a more particular revelation. "He who has seen me has seen the Father." God may have other self-disclosures in religions other than Christianity, but the church tradition is concerned primarily with God's self-disclosure in the Old and New Testaments and in Jesus Christ. ◀

▶ I cannot confess faith in God without claiming that in the narrative of Jesus of Nazareth we find our clearest parable of God. In fact, to confess faith in God for the Christian is to declare by words and life that Jesus Christ is the self-enacted parable of God. It is the narrative of his life and teaching that gives us the power to recognize God elsewhere. We can see the pattern of God for us outside of Christianity, yet we cannot but confess and profess and tell the parable of his life, passion, death, and resurrection. This is precisely what allows us to recognize God's presence and intent elsewhere than in the Christian tradition. Taking Jesus as the definitive parable of God means recognizing the rule and presence of God wherever justice and compassion are displayed. ◄

CHRIST'S AUTHORITY AS INVITATION

For many Christians, then, it appears that the order of the argument is not, "Jesus is God, so pay attention to him," but rather, "Look at Jesus, and see whether he might be God."

► The greatest authority of Christ continues to be for me not what the theologians abstractly say he is, but above all the goodness, the simple directness, the strong yet vulnerable man without self-pity that comes through the biblical accounts of his life and action. His openness and acceptance of all kinds of persons, his going to the heart of matters, his knowledge of how to rebuild his own inner resources when depleted—all of these speak of so whole and collected a human being that one never ceases to wonder at his appearance among us.

When recommending this Christ to those who are seeking, I invite them to examine the directness of this man's life and words (a deceptive directness, it is true). How can we comprehend the potential of human beings, and how can we know the extent of God's claim on us apart from this Jesus? There is so great a richness in this person and in the variety and depth of responses to him across the centuries that the richness seems inexhaustible. All of the richness is dependent upon the relationship with God the Creator and God as Spirit, so I am recommending to others not simply a good man, but one who demonstrates to us in a unique way the nature of God—and not only God in him or herself, but God-for-us.

A crucial ingredient of that understanding of God-for-us is that it happens in history. Christian faith is not a bridge out of this evil world. Jesus said in the garden to his disciples, "Remain here and watch." The central image is a cross, not a bridge. The cross stands for encounter and conflict and painful resolution. It is the place where love is practiced and understood. ◄

This way of going about a Christian confession is subtly different from another, more common way. Instead of proclaiming Christ to others, it invites me to Christ. This way puts the confessor as much on the spot as the confession. It starts from a quiet recognition that Christ did not ask us to figure out whether Christianity is superior to other religions, but asked us whether we love him. Some of those who hesitate to say yes to Christ's question may simply be unsure about the truth of his claims. To such people, this confession extends an invitation to taste and try before they decide—a step of "I believe, but help my unbelief." Others who hesitate to say yes may simply be unsure not about Christ, but about themselves; they are afraid of failing, and so sink before they swim. "We feel we could die for Christ, but can we live for him in the way he asks?" This confession invites such people to taste and try, at least try to see in Christ a possible answer about whether they can do it.

How, then, does Christ actually get confessed? How does Christ actually work in the life of faith of Christians?

Claire Hahn, with the honesty and clarity forced on her

by drastic illness, refused to sentimentalize Christ. If he was to be any comfort to her, it would not be easy comfort. "God was kind to Jesus because God's Son is God's kind of folks." When Christ's divinity is confessed in so striking a way, it becomes clear that his humanity, his "being tempted in all things as we are," is the only guard against his becoming a terror and a torment to us.

▶ I believe in God. I have faith in God. In my better moments I genuinely trust in God. Why? I read the Bible, and most of the time what it says grips me in a compelling way, not unlike but more consistently than other stories. This is especially true when I encounter the person of Jesus, whose teaching and conduct challenge and encourage me. ◀

▶ When I receive Christ in Holy Communion, I believe Christ nourishes and strengthens me. But it is also the Christ in Communion who challenges me to be his presence in the world. I recall the words of Pope John XXIII, "Remember that Christ's eighth sacrament is you," and of Saint Augustine who said regarding the Eucharist, "Receive what you are; become what you receive." The Christ I receive in Communion calls me to treat other women and men as my sisters and brothers. Christ is present in Communion to encourage me so that I might recognize him later in the challenge of the hungry, the thirsty, the naked, the sick, the imprisoned, and the homeless. ◀

The challenge of Christ without the encouragement would likely paralyze us. The encouragement of Christ without the challenge would likely make us into nice, bland, self-satisfied people. When the challenge and the encouragement are operating together, the story of Jesus can be both a guide to where we should go and a means of making sense of where we have been. This happened for a church study group and for an elderly man.

▶ We began to consider in greater depth the evidence from Scripture of Jesus' example and experience of being constantly in relationship with the Father, such as "I and the Father are one." In our efforts to come closer to Jesus, we may miss the example he set for us in his ongoing relationship with the Father. To whomever we pray, we might follow Jesus' example of an active and relational sort of prayer experience. Several in the group had difficulties with this idea because they had no personal experience of it, but the group accepted it as an ideal toward which we strive. ◀

▶ Now, at age seventy, I reflect on the meaning of my life story as a whole. But I cannot comprehend my story or any story without knowing the beginning and the end. Yet I am always in the middle. But that is where vocation or calling comes in. In my own story, my vocation comes from God and leads me toward God. The center is Christ: it is his passion which is in the middle. This takes me to the center of my own story. God is not the God of any unless the God of all, and my story is not authentic unless it is part of the total story, which is God's story. As Paul says, the only thing that matters is a new creation, and the new creation comes in the Bible at the point of crucifixion: the crucifixion of Jesus, of the world, and of me. ◀

The confessional way of "doing" the doctrine of Christ can get Christians out of the either-or trap. In the new context created by the act of confessing my faith, I may get beyond the impasse of uneasy conscience that can arise when I try to claim that faith for everyone. If I cannot prove to others that Christ is Lord and Savior of all, I still can confess to others that centrality of Christ. I still can confess who I believe I am before God. And Christ's centrality becomes the heart of my understanding others, the ground and guarantee of my ability to respect the world's quite different ways of confessing faiths other than Christian.

▶ I went to human experience of unmerited and wide-spread ethnic suffering. I found all the Christologies insufficient. In other religions and in Christian theology as it is being developed in Africa, I found something of a source. For me, Christ is the center but no longer the circumference of God's revelation. I pay greater attention to the way God works in history. There is no special sacred history, but only world history. Christ Jesus is not only the reconciler, but the liberator as well, and this points to God's concern with the dignity and wholeness of the human condition, as distinguished from merely individual salvation. ◀

FIRST PERSON PLURAL

Confessing faith creates a new context for the doctrine of Christ. The act of confessing itself thrives in a context which is not especially familiar in most of the Christian churches in America: the first person plural. The notion of individual salvation comes easily to us, because it fits so neatly with our traditions of individual freedom and responsibility. People who characteristically use "we" rather than "I" create dissonances with our culture.

▶ I want to write and understand in the first person plural more than the singular—we, not I. While Christ as incarnation may initially overwhelm us in the personal realm (since we as individuals know best our own unworthiness), Christ remains clearly revealed for more than the "me" of each of us.

Further, that "we-feeling" connects me with more than those immediately present or within reach. It propels me into an entire world of sisters and brothers. Some I know better than others as related through Christ, but many of them I am compelled to acknowledge because of Christ's message and its universal scope. Many of them I also question: because of the human strings attached, their confessing acts contradict my understanding of that universal message. ◄

► The center of my faith, where I find both Christ and a community deserving the word "church," is the Eucharist. This meal conveys so very much: God's feeding our deepest hungers, a party that brings a family alive, and the whole story of Jesus' last supper, passion, death, and resurrection. It has become, over the years, my epitome of Christian faith—the enactment of Scripture, tradition, and sacrament that presses everything together. Above all, though, it is bread of life: hope, strength to go on, reason for raising a cheer. I'm never more myself and more connected to the rest of Christ's body than at the peaceful center of my little church's Eucharist. ◄

The first person plural in the whole body of Christ hardly seems characteristic of most American Christians. Neither does the patience that is required for a lifetime's seeking to confess faith in God. We would rather say we found it than that we are looking for it.

► I see God as revealed most perfectly in Jesus Christ. Hence, my understanding of and commitment to confessing faith in God today is a matter of progressive identification, in spite of failure, with the person and message of Jesus embodied in Scripture and the life of the church.

Central to my confessing faith is the Gospel account of Jesus calling a body of believers into being on the basis of faith in him, a faith expressed freely if very imperfectly in their following. Progressively, by this gift of self and in spite of personal limitations and infidelities, these believers come to accept him as Savior and to perceive the meaning of their lives as being a living out of the life he made possible.

I believe that central to their Christian lives and hence to mine, if it is to be a life of Christian faith, are the commitments alluded to in Acts 2 and 4: participation in prayer, in the life and worship of the temple, in the breaking of the bread; concern for the teaching of the Word; an open sharing with and sustaining of others according to their needs. That sharing and sustaining must be conceived on as wide a range as Christ's own—the poor, the sinners, the outcasts of all times. And confessing faith commits me somehow to do as Jesus did in himself and in his service: preserve the mystery in incarnating it, and preserve an astonishing earthiness while transcending it. ◀

Do we American Christians not need a livelier sense of community—more "we," less "I," and more patience: the apostolic commitments to prayer, worship, breaking bread, teaching, sharing, sustaining—if we are to confess our faith with energy and confidence? Do we not also need more imagination?

▶ Jesus is central to Christian faith, but so much of our talk about Jesus is tired and flabby that we are tempted to place him aside. Perhaps poetic approaches to Jesus rather than literal ones would freshen our doctrine of Christ and make our confessing of Jesus appropriately alert.

Poetic approaches could also undercut the literalistic

abuses of Jesus' maleness. I cannot countenance a Jesus whose maleness forbids ordination to women. On the other hand, I have no desire to abandon Jesus for such feminist deities as the Great Mother or to replace christological confessions with *wicca* rites of kissing trees. Rather, I want a Jesus whose humanity challenges, excites, educates, and comforts my own, and a Jesus whose divinity is his revelation of God's surpassing goodness. I suspect such a Jesus is more than available if we can summon the wit to hear him. ◀

SAYING AND HEARING

The statement which opened this chapter has kept bringing us back to the question of the place of Christ in confessing faith in God. "God works outside the tradition—and we in the church should be glad of that." "I used to be very outspoken, but now I am more gentle, and am even dubious about loud Christians who seem to know all the answers."

▶ My own affirmation and understanding are never adequate. Only a genuine listening to how other Christians have experienced the Word of God to them, and how non-Christians have listened to the Word of God to them, can make my own understanding of God's Word authentic. My doctrine of Christ is decisive, and for just that reason it includes all people, excludes none. ◀

We circle back to the question once more and find it transposed into a new key: the uniqueness of Christ is not an abstract issue, but something alive in your uniqueness and mine. For her, confessing God is possible only through confessing Christ; for him, it is only in confessing God that

Christ is revealed as the Way; for these, Christ is a teacher and model of confessing; for those, Christ is not known or recognized in the act of confessing God. We try to understand when to speak and when to listen. We try not to time things according to our impatience or to have everything settled before it can be settled well. "We do not read anyone out of salvation." We try to confess faithfully and to remember that everyone has something important to say, and everyone has something important to hear.

5

Formation, De-Formation, Re-Formation

"In response to God's love, my confessing is a striving for simplicities in a complex world without fooling myself." Why is this so hard to do?

The complexity of today's world has a lot to do with it. "My experience has been scattered; how can I make real sense of it?" "The complexity of life drives people to simple, quick answers. We give up control of our lives to impersonal 'decision-making' by others because it is just too complicated to sort out. The major response most of us seem able to summon up is no, but so often it is no to less than a real enemy; it's no to a scapegoat designated by bigots or leaders unwilling to take responsibility for their actions or failure to act."

The complexity of the world does account for some of our difficulty, but people in other times and places have also had to try to make sense of a baffling world. For us, the real sting is in the suspicion that we are fooling ourselves. Our age is known as one of anxiety; even more, an age of suspicion. We have become experts at smoking out others' hidden agendas, and even our own. "I am so attentive to my own motivations that the likelihood of a spontaneous, genuine action by myself or by others disappears."

Many people judge that traditional theology is vaguely unreal and doesn't clarify their needed, genuine "simplicities in a complex world." One reason for this is that theologians, like other professionals, develop language patterns that drift away from common speech. But there is a deeper reason. Much theological speculation is carried on in virtual isolation from those religious realities which most Christians experience. "When theologians talk, they talk as if they had God in the hand. The average person struggles. I am amazed at the facility with which we speak of God."

Theology has continued to take its bearings from philosophy, while our entire culture has been taught to think in psychological terms. Psychology suggests that the way we confess faith in God is often conditioned more by how we have been brought up than by what theologians tell us we can and cannot believe. Our spirits are being shaped and formed all the time, whether we are conscious of it or not, and we fear fooling ourselves because we are aware (even if we wouldn't put it this way) that our spirits have some knots and twists in them that can choke and strain our confession of faith in God.

Ideally, our spirits grow toward the stature of the fullness of Christ. All too often, however, the spiritual formation we actually experience de-forms us. We like to think we can put the past completely behind us, but we are creatures of habit well beyond the limits we would care to admit. We retain ways of thinking, feeling, and acting from our earlier formation, even when they are harmful. We haven't the patience it takes to re-form. "When the people saw that Moses delayed to come down from the mountain, the people gathered themselves together to Aaron, and said to him, 'Up, make us gods, who shall go before us; as for this Moses, the man who brought us up out of the land of Egypt, we do not know what has become of him'" (Ex. 32:1). A modern equivalent of that ancient complaint is the question asked by someone who thinks salvation has been oversold, "Where is this new person I am supposed to be?"

"I am intimidated by the risk, or rather the likelihood, that my motives, values, and priorities will be misunderstood in direct proportion to the degree I pursue them in my life of faith." We worry about others misunderstanding us. We worry more that we will misinterpret our own motives.

▶ At the end of my sophomore year in college I was returning home by plane. A fellow student, looking out the window, said to me, "Just look at all those people down there knee-deep in the little messes they call their lives!" I admired this as a sophisticated, educated observation, one of those insights we were in college to get. After landing, on the way home, I mentioned the remark to my parents, confidently expecting them to be impressed. My father fixed me with a stern eye, and said, "Yes, but they're doing the best they can with what they have."

Several years later, marital crisis taught me that much education and trained rational insights still left me incapable of dealing with many parts of my life. I found out that I, like "all those people down there," had to "do the best I could with what I had." ◀

Formation, which so easily twists into de-formation, happens to us at many levels. In order to think about formation, we have to separate out strands which in our experience are all tied up with each other: psychological, religious, and cultural. With so many chances to be fooled —by ourselves, by our church, by our society—it is little wonder we would just as soon forget about confessing faith in God and get on with the business of getting and spending and pursuing happiness.

PSYCHOLOGICAL FORMATION

Two autobiographical reflections show how psychological formation can go awry and how difficult re-formation can be.

▶ Viewed from one perspective, much of my life has been a nay saying. A pietistic church nurtured in me a carefulness for behavior and appearance and a repression of emotion. These attitudes were furthered in me also by a strait-laced college and by a lifelong reaction to profligate squandering of life and resource by an alcoholic father and sister.

This does not mean that passion is absent, but it is often intolerably controlled. We can wish that many prominent individuals in history had been more controlled, but that is little comfort to me when my sights far exceed my grasp because of a needless binding of the spirit. ◀

▶ There came a period of acute crisis over identity, and during a two-year psychotherapy I left religion, theology, Bible reading, and everything associated with them far in the background. On reflection, I now see that the process of psychotherapy amounted to a kind of salvation. I learned from the process to appreciate the importance of what might be called penultimates in life.

Ultimate concerns are theological: faith and grace. But I now see that when matters of personal identity, which are in theological terms less than ultimate, are not in good order, the ultimates are themselves at best terribly distorted; theological realities can become unbearable.

I am convinced that God was both present and not present in the process. God was not present in my consciousness or the doctor's. God was clearly present in leading me

through the process at the hands of a secularized Jew of
great skill. ◄

Most of us make only occasional, brief forays into our
inner worlds. What does a psychologist, who makes a
living at such inner searches for other people, see?

► It is a unique experience for me to express my personal
belief in God. It frightens me. My work shields me from the
need to be autobiographical.

I persist in the thought that I am a person of faith in spite
of the fact that I have made no conscious effort to seek faith
or preserve faith. My chosen quest in and of itself is quite
indifferent to belief as such. I am as willing to be led into
unbelief as belief. I grant that belief would be more com-
forting, more attractive, secure, less frightening and less
lonely.

The persistent quest is into the dark and elusive (seemingly unassailable at times) fortress on the inside of human
beings. The realm of the unconscious is peopled by the
most primitive devils and the most unreligious impulses. I
am reminded and sobered by Freud's statement, "No one
like me who presumes to wrestle with the dark forces
within can hope to come through the struggle unscathed."
At the same time, I am encouraged by the image of Jacob's
wrestling with God.

My wife laughs with genuine empathy (and even a little
admiration, I think) at what she calls my "complete dedication to the inner search." The continuity of the search
seems to be inspired, directed, and paced by a statement
from John's Gospel which I embraced years ago as a word
of life: "The truth shall make you free." I consider this a
most radically valid psychic insight. This forms the central
church tradition for me.

At times I am very conscious of a merely halfhearted

desire to be free—even an aversion to it. At this moment, as I reflect on it, I am repulsed by the lowly, separate, and dangerous aspects of freedom.

Always I am conscious of the limitedness of the outcome —the finiteness of my ability to comprehend the truth. I cannot contain the truth; I only hope to approach it, sandals in hand.

Although I am all I have been given to know and direct, the quest should not lead inward to a dead end and sterility. This would be to miss the mark completely—a psychic suicide and a nonquest. The search for truth draws one inevitably through oneself (past the monumental insignificance, the petty rage) to others.

I have never admitted to anyone that I pray daily. Each day I recall and face myself with the words of Jesus, "Whatever you do to one of these my brethren, you do to me."

If I were to codify in some manner what faith means to me, the propositions would flow from the above two biblical statements:

1. Faith is the faith of persons (not merely a cumulative tradition).
2. Faith is relational (interpersonal).
3. Faith is personal and subjective (intrapersonal).
4. Every faith is an experience of, response and commitment to, ultimate reality in a specific historical situation.
5. Faith of necessity is syncretistic (it absorbs and assimilates numerous experiences).
6. All faith changes and is in process.
7. Faith is an integrative attempt.
8. The human being is a religious being.
9. Faith raises the question of a religious drive. ◀

We long for freedom to be whole persons, but when we look that freedom in the face, when we see how God's offer of freedom puts us on the spot, our desire for freedom becomes halfhearted, we shy away, are perhaps even repulsed. "There are many so-called atheists who exhibit faith and people who believe in God who don't. It is easy to see why the early pioneers in psychoanalysis said that religion is only a projection."

▶ Some psychiatrists report that people who dedicate themselves to religious faith and to God fall into two broad categories: either depression or schizophrenia. Other psychiatrists find this utterly simple-minded, but the claim does pose a question about the relation between psychological conditions and the confession of faith.

Confessing God might always be subject to abuse: it can be a cover-up or a way of dealing with depression or schizophrenia; but this cannot be a way of defining the relationship between psychological conditions and confessing faith. What, then, about the role of brokenness, partiality, and even lack of psychological integration as a factor in confessing faith? Do the extremes of this condition actually prevent confessing faith?

If our self-esteem is low, our capacity to confess God is diminished. People who come to a basic self-affirmation seem better enabled to confess God. But then, is it easier to confess God in the face of good times and conditions or of difficult times and conditions? The answer is yes or no, depending upon how the question originates for us. Surely we cannot say that being aware of God depends on good things happening. Yet crises are not always productive of confessing faith in God either.

So we are led to ask: Does conversion create the conditions of self-worth? Or does self-worth have to be already in place before one can turn to God?

There is no easy answer—and that itself is a key insight into the issues which face us. If we are confessing faith in a

God who has made a covenant with human beings, then we have been given responsibility for alleviating conditions which constrict and diminish human awareness of the mystery and wonder in life. We cannot conclude from this, however, that if we remove psychological, social, economic, and other barriers which prevent free response to God, we are necessarily going to make it easier to confess God.

We must therefore be careful not to be too sure that we know who is and who is not in a position to confess authentic faith. ◀

Indeed, we cannot be sure what the conditions are. But there is one set of conditions that makes even the first stirrings of faith in the true God almost impossible.

▶ I find that many people have no real experience of having faith in anyone, hoping in anyone, or loving anyone. There is no experience of the common grace of the everyday. Therefore, the true God can't even be brought into their consciousness. This lack of deep trust spreads to a distrust of everything. There has to be a decisive experience of trust in someone and of being with someone to be able even to see the decisiveness of Christ. ◀

▶ From my standpoint as a Christian, an ordained clergyperson, and a therapist, I believe God has already said yes to the human condition in Jesus. I also believe therapy is one way in which a sense of God's radical acceptance, forgiveness, and grace can be made known in a life demoralized by rejection or paralyzed by guilt and fear.

A young woman came to find out whether there was any hope of saving her marriage. Her husband had quit his business and had moved in with another woman. He indicated early on that he wasn't interested in therapy. Survival issues, both physical and emotional, dominated the woman's therapy sessions.

She felt she was without worth. She was rejected and abandoned by her husband. She believed she had no marketable skills. Soon she began to blame herself for the failure of the marriage, and she felt inadequate because she was too fearful to go and search for a job.

Her pastor and I were able to provide the encouragement and psychic support she needed to make critical decisions about her children, her home, her changed social life, and her faith.

In therapy she was able to sort out feelings and distortions from facts. At first she was very unsure of herself and wondered if she were going crazy. She did not appreciate the tremendous burden the marital breakup had thrust on her.

She terminated therapy, and then returned a few weeks later, saying she wasn't as strong as she had thought. She felt she had failed her therapist and herself.

This second time she was able to go deeper than survival issues. She was ready to confront more squarely the depth of her rage and of her faith in a loving and forgiving God. She felt God's love as a sustaining presence; after all, it had brought her this far. But she was deeply angry and enraged and felt that was wrong, a sign of ingratitude. She thought her anger showed a lack of faith.

She then asked: "Is it possible to be so angry and still be a Christian?" I assured her that it was, that she should acknowledge just how deeply hurt she felt, and that her rage was one way in which she could tell herself that she was important and then discover an inner letting-go, an exorcism, and eventually a freedom from self-blame. Her rage may also be interpreted as a form of prayer, a deep cry and reaching out—in a hope that words may not be able to express.

When she was in deepest pain I prayed for her and for our work together. At the heart of the Christian faith is the experience that God cares and accepts us as we are. It is up to people to convey this sense of underlying care to each other. As she worked through her hurt, pain, and rage, she was able to move beyond her sorrow songs and to sing songs of joy with new vitality. ◀

RELIGIOUS FORMATION

We expect the common grace of the everyday to be made real in our churches, and of course it can be found there. To an alarming degree, however, the churches reinforce the problem. Our suspicion of our psychological formation, our fear that we may be tricking ourselves, goes hand in hand with our distrust of our religious formation.

▶ I was graced with a nurturing that made the confession of faith in God the most important thing in my life. But it was riddled with half-truths, untruths, evasions, equivocations, and romanticisms that vitiated its permanent value. As I knew more, cared more, took a larger responsibility, aspects of that earlier nurturing collapsed. Not everyone has to go through this, and I claim no elitist privilege for those whose style and opportunities make it happen. But because of my own history, I care especially about those who have to face this happening. I care about them not at the expense of others who need caring for, but as an instinctive priority; this is the case about which I know best and the one I have taken most pains to fit myself to meet.

I represent not the liberal or liberated confessors, but those who already harbor an uneasy suspicion that we ought to agree not to look at things too closely for fear that they will collapse, and those who currently enjoy a happy confidence that is bound to disintegrate as they look more closely. My project is to protect for them an authentic and authoritative confession that will stand in all weather. I do not insist on imposing such a confession on everyone. I do insist on making it available for those who require it. ◀

For many Christians the questions are pointed and painful: "Is the formation which I can no longer own, which I must reject if I am to be honest before myself, others, and even before God, itself the norm of Christian faith?" "What am I to make of the fact that I was catechized but not converted, and that now, when I have a strong sense of being converted, I find myself forgetting the catechism?" "Am I rejecting the faith or simply leaving the church?" "I had to get out of my church in order to preserve my faith." "Are all people of real faith heretics at heart?"

If we insist on faith in God as a definite package deal which we either take or leave, many serious people will leave it. But if we take our bearings from those students of human behavior who understand our stages of identity and moral formation, we will recognize that maturing in faith is what we are called to, not what we are warned against. Such maturing can take place in many ways, even apparently opposite ones.

▶ I had some very pious neighbors in my early childhood—the holier-than-thou kind—who strongly influenced my mother and our small local church. They almost ruined religion for me. Later, in college, I was exposed to a campus ministry that made me realize Christianity was much broader in scope than I had thought. That opened the door for me to begin thinking about it again. ◀

▶ I grew up in a church which allowed great latitude to the

mind, and college and graduate school furthered my intellectual grasp of the Christian tradition. In the process, religion almost disappeared for me. It was the rediscovery of the local church with its variety of people, its balanced appreciation and suspicion of academic abstraction, its reminder that while Christianity is broad in its scope it is also deep in its probings of the human heart, that opened the way for me to begin being an active Christian again. ◀

The church can hinder genuine growth in faith in many ways. The church can be too rigid.

▶ Confessing faith in God today is confused by the entrenched positions of those in church and society who have very limited concepts of what can be confessed; these narrow notions not only limit the range of potential hearers, they confuse me as well. ◀

The church can be too bland and vague.

▶ A certain casualness pervades the churches, a folksiness born not out of genuine roots in rural America, but often in a middle-class friendliness, a sincere belief that being nice and warmhearted is the highest Christian virtue, or that a bright smile is the proper profile of a true confessing Christian. When scriptural holiness is watered down to proper etiquette, faith becomes a way of avoiding the gospel's deeper encounter with suffering and evil. ◀

The church can be too dull.

▶ Worship is often not the powerful experience of the risen Lord. Sometimes the Sunday congregation seems to be "God's frozen people," and worship is an hour to be

dutifully endured rather than eagerly anticipated. Since
worship is by definition a celebration of faith, good celebrations enhance faith, bad celebrations diminish it. ◄

The church can be too familiar.

► The danger today comes from groups of people confessing a similar testimony and forming themselves into
tightknit, homogeneous groups where all truth is judged
by the yardstick of one particular experience. It is only
in the company of others very unlike ourselves that we
have the checks and balances to see our own testimony in
perspective. ◄

The church can be too shortsighted.

► The local is not real if it is only local. There is a tone of
unreality in a merely local community which ignores what
and who are beyond the local. ◄

The church can be insensitive.

► Most Christian churches have abused half their con-
stituency—women—and continue to do so today. A mas-
culine God is sexism at the core of Christian faith. A refusal
to grant women equal access to church power—and not
just access in theory, but in practice—is sexism that cuts
away the church's religious authority from its roots. Only
when the church wholly defeats the Paul of 1 Cor. 14:34
("the women should keep silence in the churches") by the
Paul of Gal. 3:28 ("there is neither Jew nor Greek, there is
neither slave nor free, there is neither male nor female; for
you are all one in Christ Jesus") will church witness be
credible. Until a woman can be pope or archbishop, the

church will not merit the full hearing of persons liberated from sexism. ◀

Cataloguing ways in which churches de-form us is not a pastime for people who couldn't care less. On the contrary, it is a heartfelt cry from persons who passionately want a spiritual formation that will stand up in all weather, or at least one that will not make us run for cover when the first clouds appear on the horizon; who want, indeed, a faith in God that will create weather patterns on its own.

▶ When we are dealing with God or even just with our own faith in God, we are in an arena which is beyond complete rational understanding. If I were to talk about "stating" or "asserting" my faith in God, you might think I was very sure of myself and my understanding. Somehow, "confess" has a different feeling. It is not just an intellectual exercise. Confession seems to come from inside somewhere—not just from the head.

I can try to confess my faith, knowing how inadequate my faith is, and also how very inadequate my means of expression are in dealing with so overwhelming a fact as my relationship to God. I guess an intellectual statement could be made which would not require any coherence with feeling. Confessing faith means I must find a way to express a feeling which includes an idea but is much more than that. ◀

▶ A prime part of my confessing faith in God is the talking to God, the quiet being with God that my Roman Catholic tradition has encouraged. Contemplation, meditation, silent prayer: the names matter little, but the reality feeds my spirit.

In the quiet of the early morning, I try to center in God's

presence, to hear the love that holds me. My own responding voice sometimes is strident with pain; at other times it is soft with gratitude. Either way, I've learned that these minutes are a precious time just to be myself in God's presence: nonprofit, unfocused, with neither goal nor schedule—a blessed free zone for touching base with the one reality that never fails.

By making time for this prayer most days, I've been able slowly to increase the number of daily affairs I refer to God in work times, when my individual faith merges with that of the larger community. So, with many failings but also much hope, I have started to glimpse something of God's deepest grace, the ever-present divine love. ◄

There is a deep-seated conviction in American Christianity that what is really serious about religion is either in the conscious mind or in purely personal experience. Sacraments and liturgies, rites and myths are significant only to the extent that they can be explained in a way satisfactory to the mind's demands or justified as aids to individual piety.

► In my tradition, because of its excessive emphasis on experience as a criterion for authenticity of faith, there has been relatively little awareness of the formative power of good liturgy. In addition, we have lacked exposure to the riches of the larger traditions and forms of Christian life and experience. We thus reap the harvest of generations of little or no education for worship. The divorce between personal piety and corporate worship on the one hand and between theology and prayer on the other makes it difficult to proclaim the intimate link between liturgy and life, communal celebration and mission, and above all, to uncover the essential mystery of the church's life in dying and rising with Christ. ◄

Anything not rational is dismissed as magic. "People have trouble verbalizing any feelings" because feelings are suspected of being slightly subhuman. "I believed that decisions could be made only rationally. But my wife operated intuitively, and I learned that she could be right!" Christianity has had "a tendency to assume too direct a relation between human formulations of belief and the realities to which they point, and hence to define Christian witness too much in terms of belief and not enough in terms of style of life and works." "We in the West are hooked on the notion that all our knowing is mental. Asia and Africa know better; our confessing of God must concern not just the spiritual (which we interpret as mental), but the whole person. I am disturbed that so much of our theology is addressed, in effect, to nonpersons." We miss the main point when, in an effort to do honor to God, we say that "our faith must be on a higher plane than our everyday style of living."

In worship, the Christian churches have an antidote to this habit of treating people as disembodied spirits. Is it commonly but erroneously thought that the worship of God is an activity with little if any grip on the real world?

▶ Worship and ethics were not seen in the early church as cause and effect or as inner and outer manifestations of faith. What was remembered and enacted in the gathering for worship was continuous with what was confessed in the lives of martyrs and ordinary believers. This is not to say that the gap between the ideal and the actual was not recognized in Corinth, Galatia, and elsewhere. But it was understood that worship and ethics together expressed faithfulness to Jesus as Lord. ◀

The antidote could be much more effective if we would let it.

▶ I have learned how Protestants and Orthodox understand worship differently from the way I do. But as a Catholic I am distressed to find that we cannot discuss our differences frankly and fully in an effort to make them complementary rather than divisive. Worship is essentially that lift of the Spirit without which confession is verbiage or activist distraction. There is no healthy church life without a deep liturgy or communal prayer that flows back and forth with practical service. Our ability to worship together has filled me with hope that one day we will be a church united. Our inability to work through our differences on worship has shown me that this church united is a long way off. ◀

▶ Worship is withdrawing from or transcending everydayishness, and especially that aspect of the everyday which places my self in the center of events. Worship's goal is the expansion of the self to the point of a combined communion or identity with creation and its source and sustenance.

The process for me includes four stages: a centering, a purgation or self-emptying, illumination or revelation, and union which is a state of grace and communion.

Christians go about worship in very different ways. While many people find it is worship that gets us beyond barriers and unifies us, this is only partially true for me. Although the action of worship can bring community, it often does not and simply leaves Christians of different traditions more aware of the radically different ways in which they experience God. My own most intense experiences of unity with other Christians of different churches have come in actions in the world—working together to relieve suffering and bring justice. ◀

Worship, which would be so much more effective if we

could really do it together, reminds us that we are not just our minds or just our bodies, but whole persons intricately woven together and fashioned out of ideas, emotions, motives, instincts, upbringing, hopes, doubts, sins, good deeds, blindness, vision. Worship draws us into a drama which carries us through and beyond the neat categories we construct for ourselves—this is a secular matter and this is a spiritual one, or this is about my body and this is about my soul. Worship can put the shattered Humpty Dumpty of our experience together again. In worship we may come closer than anywhere else to achieving the longed-for, terribly elusive goal of spontaneity.

Such spontaneity is vividly present in the American black churches, whose wealth of insight and understanding is almost totally unknown to the majority of other American Christians. The rest of us could learn a great deal from black Christians about ways in which the church can form persons positively to confess their faith in God.

▶ When I say God, what do I really mean? My first idea came from the context of the black church. God was never experienced apart from that church experience. God is real in the sense that the world will disappear from me if you take away the cultural situation in which I experience God.

In the black church, God was understood. We didn't have to unravel God; God came out of the understanding which bound us together. A case in point is my understanding of prayer. I experience prayer when the community is supportive and concentrating on a tragic or joyful event which has happened. In our home, there is God. ◀

▶ Those who nurtured my faith were largely unlettered, including my mother and father. From an early age I simply assumed God and church. During my pilgrimage as a black Christian through high school, college, and graduate school, the presence of God has been an abiding reality.

Like Moses I have stood at the Red Sea and wondered *when* it will open. I had no doubt *that* it would open, but like Moses, I only waited for it to open at the right time—just when I needed it most. Through success and failure, God is real to me. In fact, what the world calls failure may not be if I have been loyal to the royal within me. ◄

CULTURAL FORMATION

Just as awareness of our own mixed motives can paralyze us and distrust of our religious formation can enrage us, so the catalog of cultural de-formations can numb us. Many Christians in North America are so caught up in the society's values that is is hard for them to hear the sharp challenge posed by many of those values to authentic faith in God. The assumptions of a culture which is mostly indifferent to Christian tradition and frequently opposed to it lie deep within those of us who profess to believe, and we may not even be aware that culture has any bearing on faith in God. We may have assigned faith a small compartment in an already crowded life. That is why a personal starting point is essential: the question is not at arm's length and abstract—"How can Americans confess faith in God?"—but intimate and concrete—"How can I confess faith in God?"

Most of American society is geared to instant gratification. This is reflected in the widespread assumption that confessing faith in God means good feelings, being happy, solving problems, the certainty that one is going to blessed eternal life. There is little in current American culture that encourages the development of a disciplined spiritual life, a seeking of God over a long period of time through rough and dark places as well as through smooth and light ones.

Such a seeking—tempered by difficulty and doubt, prepared for frustration and for times when confessing faith in God makes us acutely unhappy—is authentically Christian and at odds with much in our society and in our churches.

Living from moment to moment and lurching from crisis to crisis, as we seem to be doing both as individuals and as a people, is evidence of confusion at a deep level—the confusion of those who are uncertain of their very identity. The traditional principles which gave our society a sense of identity have lost their credibility and their power to integrate. In this condition national purpose remains vague, and the nation leaves fateful problems unaddressed not for lack of know-how or money, but for lack of will and purpose.

▶ As a young American Christian I learned that my religion and my national heritage converged in a regard for the sacredness and dignity of humanity that was unparalleled in human affairs. Whereas other religions were otherworldly and often life denying, Christianity worshiped a God who had created all human beings in the divine image and valued them enough to die for them. That God, moreover, was a God of history who was bringing about conditions of dignity and equality and freedom, especially through agents such as the United States. The American Revolution constituted a new and momentous chapter in the movement of history toward the kingdom of God. I was proud to be a Christian whose nation had introduced a beacon of liberty into the world and was the home of European and Asian refugees, the cradle of opportunity for the lowliest, and even the defender of freedom abroad in the world wars.

Disillusionment was bound to come. Christianity, I was to learn, has not taken very seriously the implications of its universal monotheism. If Christianity had introduced into the world a new regard for human life and dignity, it had quickly learned how to justify on myriad grounds the forfeiture of human rights including the right to life. Indeed, among major world religions its death-dealing would be hard to match. Christians have justified capital punishment for heretics, witches, and virtually anyone who was disrespectful of the prevailing cultural Christianity. Pogroms against Jews, Muslims, and native Americans were regularly tolerated and supported. Christian silence and complicity in the Holocaust were thoroughly predictable. And Christians were taught until recent decades that killing in warfare was a religious duty not to be questioned on the basis of individual Christians' concepts of right and justice. ◀

At the same time that this inner confusion is prominent, the energy of the American people remains undiminished. Our society is not tired. Its energy is expended, as in the past, largely in that production of goods and services which has resulted in the present massive consumerism, which is fast drifting into a pursuit of pleasure. The justification we give for consumerism is not, as it once was, to get ahead, but to enjoy, to indulge in what is pleasant and pleasurable, and to do your own thing. The nation seems to be struggling less for something new and to be settling more for the gratifications of pleasure.

There lurks a fear of the future: where is it all leading? Yet this apprehensiveness remains vague and, in spite of warnings from a few, has produced neither a reexamination of the nation's purpose nor an evaluation of the effect of its social structure upon other nations and peoples.

There is certainly much in our current malaise that is peculiar to the urbanized West. We have persuaded ourselves that our highly developed analytical skills and our ready access to mountains of information give us a special corner on understanding and wisdom, but we do not understand what we do to the rest of the world, and we do not recognize how much we can learn about confessing faith in God from people who are very different from us.

▶ For a confession of faith to be authentic, it will have to be confession to and about the world in which we live. And that will be difficult for us Americans, including us American Christians, to do because by and large we don't really know the world we live in, though every once in a while a few haunting facts get our attention for a few moments:

* In this world, 15,000 people die of hunger every day.
* Less than one percent of this world's peoples now live under colonial governments. No longer must these people work for someone else's visions, for someone else's goals.
* If this world were a village of 100 people, one-third would be rich, two-thirds poor. Six would be Americans possessing one-third of the village's total income, and the remaining ninety-four would sit outside the picture window and watch them spend it.
* In 1900, eighty-five percent of the Christian population of the world was centered in Europe and North America. If present demographic trends continue, however, by the year 2000 fifty-eight percent of the world's Christians will live in the Third World. Moreover, although thirty-four percent of the world was Christian in 1900, by the year 2000—given these same developments—only sixteen percent may be any kind of Christian at all.
* In the face of all this, the United States, a nation deeply shaped by the Christian tradition, has vowed to defend its oil fields in the Middle East. The question is not whether we'll be a sign, but rather what *kind* of sign will we be. ◀

These statistics are widely known, but seldom felt in all their overwhelming challenge to our faith in God. In the face of such realities, what are we to make of the titles on the best-seller lists: *Looking Out for No. 1; Winning Through Intimidation; Dress for Success?* How can we justify the way we chase after wealth, security, and happiness? "We congratulate ourselves on being advanced and say it is too much to ask us to bend to understand those not so advanced, the poor of the earth, when they come as refugees into our midst, or when they serve our tables with their stoop labor in farm fields."

Is the main reason why these facts about our world don't register in our hearts that, if they did, we would be forced to change the way we live or admit finally that our faith is not really in God? Perhaps.

There may be other reasons too, and they also are reinforced by American values. We simply haven't time in our busy schedules for the rest of the world and the God whose world it is. "We are efficient. We cannot give up the clock and the deadline or we will sink into nonproductiveness, even heaven forbid, chaos." "It is hard to perceive confessing faith in God as a significant act when there is such a multitude of options competing for my interest." But cataloging reasons may simply be a way of evading the real issue.

▶ I am impatient with attempts to explain why we remain so smug in the face of the world's needs and disorders, and why we take so little responsibility for our situation and our power to change things. Explanations, even of our smugness, too often try to make it understandable, forgivable, even justifiable. No! It can't be understood or forgiven or justified. It's too obscene, too horrible! It's not a problem, it's a monstrosity. We may keep on juggling and dickering successfully enough to get by with it all in the arena of world politics, but before the face of God nothing short of repentance and deep change can possibly be enough. ◄

The dizzying range of options makes us feel out of control, and even before the face of God we respond not with repentance and deep change, but with attempts to assert control, sometimes calculated, sometimes frenzied. "We have an obsession to control both God and others through manipulative techniques." "Our faith helps us, but first we must accept the fact that we need help."

► In our church study group discussions, we discovered that we all have difficulty in allowing God to take over when we have a problem or when we place ourselves in God's hands. It is contrary to the cultural training that places emphasis on always remaining in control. We are certain that in Christian faith we must let God be in control of our lives, yet we frequently take back the reins. ◄

Jesus said it is more blessed to give than to receive; we Americans find it easier to give than to receive. The characteristic American response to a gift is the obligation to give something in return of at least equal value. We get a gift and instinctively calculate what it will cost us to make things even again because we have an uneasy sense that a balance has been upset. Our individualism and consumerism have made even the giving of gifts into a subtle form of domination. Spontaneity in our dealings with others is rare because we suspect manipulation, and we suspect manipulation because we know ourselves as manipulators.

► When it comes to the question of service, the touchstone of Christian living, why do we of the church often say, "I know I should do more, but . . . . I don't know how to work with youth, or with refugees. I don't know their language and I feel awkward." If people lack feelings of identification, they balk at expending energy, and shrink from the unease they predict they will feel. In part, we want to be in control of situations we enter. If we do not have skills we think we need, then we will be at a disadvantage, and that is too uncomfortable. We would have to yield to the Spirit, which would make us vulnerable; and we don't like being vulnerable. ◀

The values of success, consumption, and control infect the nation and the Christians and churches within the nation in countless ways.

Some symptoms are national in their scope.

▶ When theology interprets the faith to the church, there tends to be too much emphasis on victory and triumph and success. We are not prepared for disappointment or for what is failure by ordinary standards such as defeat in Vietnam, even though authentic faith in God might make a very different judgment about what that defeat means. If God is tied directly to the nation's being "number one," then when it looks as if the nation has slipped, we retreat into a privatized faith where we can be spiritual away from public gaze. ◀

Some symptoms cover the nation, but bear down hard on particular groups.

▶ The American values are those of youth; the elderly represent the approach of death and are set aside somewhere between the ages of sixty and seventy. If they belong to the middle class, they are increasingly isolated in large retirement colonies, nursing homes, and hospitals. "Age-

ism is as virulent as sexism and racism." The elderly all too
often accept the culture's idolization of youth and fight
growing old. ◄

Some symptoms touch us in our most intimate relationships.

▶ It is easier to confess our faith when we are among
Christians who are at the same point on the road of Christianity. In many families our children, especially the
teenagers and young adults, are not necessarily at that
same point on the road where we find ourselves. Thus,
within our own family life, our witnessing becomes most
difficult. It became painful to everyone in the church study
group that those closest to us were often the most difficult
to reach. An observation concerning the Christian relationship with family is that our group avoided any in-
depth discussion on problems that may occur in confessing
or sharing our faith with our spouses. ◄

CONFESSION AND RE-FORMATION

Surrounded by so great a host of possibilities for fooling
ourselves, we are tempted to forget all about trying to
achieve any kind of simplicities in this complex world,
unless they are the simplicities of forgetfulness and pleasure. A confession of faith in God, however, calls us up
short. Our fear of fooling ourselves, it turns out, is the
biggest trick we have played on ourselves. The re-formation of the self is what faith in God is about; the
self we are afraid of fooling is the old one. The question
quoted earlier, "Where is this new person I am supposed to
be?" expresses an evident frustration, but it is the right
question.

The clue here is in the double meaning of confession.

Most people, on hearing that word immediately think of
the confession of sin, whether done to a priest in a confessional, in a group therapy session, in the liturgical
"general confession," or in private prayer. "Confessing
one's faith" involves much more than confessing sin, but if
it does not include confessing sin, it is thin and a delusion.

The biblical understanding of sin has been so torn apart
and reinterpreted that it no longer illumines the human
condition in America. In our culture of positive thinking
and pragmatism, the concept of sin has become synony-
mous with mistake or shortcoming or moral backsliding.
The idea that the nation can sin is so remote that even race
discrimination and the war in Indochina are regarded
merely as mistakes, bad judgment. It is no wonder that the
judgment of God has disappeared from view.

Sin does belong to our confession. What does this mean
for the churches' way of addressing the nation and individual Christians?

▶ The prophets and Jesus say that those who live in material, social, and religious security have their own gods and
rarely seek God with heart, mind, and soul or hear God
call. Most North Americans—that includes most of us—
live in the security of relative wealth, status, and arma-
ments—an attempted security achieved directly or indirectly at the expense of the political rights and material
well-being of many South Americans, Asians, Africans,
and possibly even of our progeny.

To confess our faith means also to confess our sins,
whether we have been conscientious about these ethical
issues or not: even the conscientious have until recently
participated unknowingly in this situation. We continue to
benefit from these quests for security as long as we are
North Americans. And most of us could be doing more.

How will this confession change me? First, it makes me admit publicly that I am to a large degree squirreled away in my bunker or safely up in my security tree. A public declaration brings clearer self-recognition and possibly helps seal off the retreats which I from time to time seek. It is either a beginning of more serious discipleship, or a revelation to myself and others that I have other gods. ◄

For many Christians, sin seems an outmoded concept, a guilt-trip largely responsible for that binding of the spirit which has made life thin and pinched. "How much do we have to dwell on seeing ourselves as sinners? Let's get on with the problem solving." "Once in a meeting about Christian missions someone reported about a people 'over there' who had no concept of guilt. Another then asked, 'How do we get those people to feel guilty so we can save them?'" The point is that we do not have to dwell on seeing ourselves as sinners; on the contrary, we see ourselves as sinners in order to be freed up to dwell on other business. Psychologists and psychiatrists specialize in freeing people from guilt, but a psychiatrist published a book called *Whatever Became of Sin?* and he did not mean good riddance. He meant that if sin is denied or disregarded, whatever psychological health is achieved will be no more than a relief of symptoms.

► I was recently in a group of ministers who did not know one another. We were introducing ourselves in the usual manner until we came to Bill. He said "I'm Bill and I'm a sinner." That blunt statement reminded me of something I had heard before.

A friend who is a member of Alcoholics Anonymous described that organization. Its openness, freedom, acceptance of each other was what I had always imagined the early church to be, and I asked him to take me to a meeting. Everybody who spoke started with, "I'm David (or Jane or Richard or Martha) and I'm an alcoholic." Many reported months or years without a drink, so after the meeting I asked my friend, "If you've been dry for some time, why keep calling yourself an alcoholic?" He replied, "Admitting that I am an alcoholic and never forgetting it is the first step toward controlling it. Second, and just as important, is admitting that I need help."

I asked the minister who had identified himself with "I'm Bill and I'm a sinner," if he was consciously echoing the AA manner of speech. He said he was, and that much of his ministry had been to Alcoholics Anonymous. He confirmed what I had sensed at the meeting I attended: by its total acceptance of people, AA comes close to the Christian ideal of the restored, forgiven community where people can be re-formed because they admit their need. They admit they are alcoholics, but do not dwell on the fact. The admission is not a guilt trip, but the precondition for getting on with the business of living. The minister confirmed also my amazement at the wonderful good humor I had sensed at the meeting; people who have few illusions about themselves have a refreshing ability not to take themselves too seriously.

Many churches offer space for weeknight AA meetings. I wonder if they understand that those meetings usually come a good deal closer to realizing the true nature of Christian community than Sunday morning worship. Worship committees are frequently under pressure from parishioners to eliminate all confession of sin from the liturgy, or at best to sandwich it in where it can be missed by someone who coughs. ◀

Faith in God calls the churches and Christians to a confession of sin not in order to lay guilt on them, but to make possible genuine repentance and forgiveness. And the process is continuous. "We may go through periods of confusion and transition in the church and in our own thinking, but there is something drastically wrong with saying, 'I will wait until I get my act together or until the church gets its house in order before I confess faith in God.' I must attempt a confession now, stammering as it might be." "I would resist a too easy identification of a Christian as one who 'gets it all together.' A Christian is sought and is a seeker, one who has been given the biblical witness and the total human experience as a means of bringing it all together. But it is not prepackaged."

WHAT ARE WE TO DO?

What are we to do, we who have done those things which we ought not to have done and have not done those things which we ought to have done? What is our calling?

▶ Sometimes I miss in my associates (and in myself) an electric sense of urgency with regard to our mission as Christians. My faith may be unauthentic because I am not in the thick of some touch-and-go battle.

Now if I should have a yen to be a less mediocre Christian and more conspicuously helpful to God, my church dishes up some cautions. By a combination of circumstances beyond my control plus my own choices, I am already somewhere—a family man and school teacher. Therefore, for authentic faith I should not presume to supersede the ethical requirement of being where I'm supposed to be at a given time and doing what I've signed up to do.

In other words, no credit accrues to me for acting like one

of God's shock troops when in fact I've been assigned quieter duties. Authentic faith therefore includes the patience to figure out not which tasks are the most dramatic, urgent, and demanding in the world, but which ones are mine. In biblical terms, whether or how much God loves me does not depend on the life station in which I find myself. ◄

"Which tasks are mine, and how do I find out?" is the question as old as the church itself. Paul had to tell the members of the body of Christ at Corinth that feet should not try to be hands and ears should not try to be eyes, but he also had to insist to those in Galatia that all the conventional distinctions—racial, sexual, and class—were no longer operative. If we suspect Paul is inconsistent here, we may not understand that persons are distinct from the roles they play.

"Our difficulty in confessing faith arises as much from role playing and the feeling of isolation as it does from more general cultural influences. We evade the intensely personal nature of confessing by the way we type ourselves, as priest, lay person, student, professor, youth, senior citizen. The diversity of gifts, not the roles we play, is the true variety of God's people." But the question pops up again, for how can I distinguish between my self and my role? "I am less convinced than others that making the most of the opportunities where I am is the answer. Does where I am insulate my self from genuine confession of faith—the tough kind?"

If I try to figure out only on my own what my tasks are, I stand a good chance of fooling myself for the whole host of reasons outlined above. But God has not called just me; God has called a people, and it is in the community with its diversity of gifts that I can search for what my tasks are. "It seems that the most effective confessing in specialized circumstance has been done by people who have come from, remain part of, and go back to stable relationships with real communities." "A disciplined spiritual life in the Christian community is the time-tested way to find out what we are to do. Discipline means I keep doing things like praying when I don't want to or when they don't make me feel good; 'in the Christian community' means that I am actively involved in the life of the institutional church even though I can think of many reasons not to be. I cannot be a member of Christ in general." "I long for a church more inclusive, more mature, more profoundly rooted in the Word and in signs of God's grace, a community in solidarity with the suffering of the world, unafraid to wrestle with the principalities and powers, willing to struggle with faith and unfaith, and eager to speak and to live the truth in love; a place where the memory and the hope are vivid ways of life, where prayer and liturgy sustain healing and prophecy, and where the kingdom may be discerned from time to time."

To "strive for simplicities in a complex world without fooling myself" is anything but simple. "I have been disillusioned with the church as an 'it.' I had to confess to the stranger God, who had once been friendly to me. I was angry. Then I began to see that God was teaching me who I was. I have learned that I do not have to cringe before God." That's finding simplicities without fooling yourself. It happened in spite of the church. That's too bad. It doesn't have to be that way.

▶ Without the help of my community, others who care about me and about things I care about, I would easily forget who I am and what I seem called to do. But now I begin to realize that the community I must listen to is much bigger than I thought, and I can't afford to hear only the voices that sound so much like my own. I will forget who I am and fail to learn what I am called to do if I don't hear voices from the other side of the tracks and the other side of the world. Only voices that are strange to me can set me straight about how deeply I misunderstand the ways of the stranger God. ◀

6
The Margins

"I am interested in reconciliation, but on a genuine basis of liberation. God through Jesus has reconciled us already, but humankind has not accepted that fact." God has made us all one, and has broken down the dividing walls of hostility, but we devote enormous resources and energy to rebuilding those walls and keeping them in good repair.

We do not accept the fact of reconciliation because reconciliation on God's terms, far from making life easy and comfortable, puts us into the rough and tumble of the world.

▶ There are no marginal people to God. Every single human being is of ultimate and eternal significance to God. The burden is on those nations, races, and sexes who have tried to keep others in subjection. We need to be ruthlessly honest—and certain that God has no preferences as to age, sex, race, economic or social condition. Whenever in any way we act as though God did have preferences, we are wrong. ◀

NO RESPECT OF PERSONS VERSUS
NO DISREGARD OF PERSONS

There are two ways to hear "God has no preferences." It could be taken to mean, "Everybody should be content with their lot, because all are equal in the sight of God." That is to substitute a laid-back, easygoing, "do-your-own-thing" deity for the Lord of heaven and earth who is confessed in the Bible. "God has no preferences" can also be taken to mean, "The goods of the earth are for all the earth's people, so that those who do not receive a fair share stand first on God's list. If we want to do God's will, we make action-lists by what we learn to be God's priorities." Some people who are serious about the Christian faith claim to find answers to ethical issues in the *Wall Street Journal* or the *New York Times.* They do not say, "We go to the Bible" or "We raise the issue in church circles." For them the church seems tongue-tied precisely at points where faith in God bears most directly on the way we live our lives.

▶ The theme of God's concern for those on the margins is not simply a nuance of faith, an extracurricular interest for those with time and leisure. A friend went through the Bible and assembled all the passages dealing with the poor and poverty. He claims that by sheer space devoted to the question, this theme is second only to idolatry.

Counting snipped verses in the Bible does not necessarily find its central themes, but I am haunted constantly by his simple, flat-footed question: Where in the systematic theologies do I find "poorology" amidst all the other "-ologies"? Should not "poorology" be at or near the center of my confession of faith in God that claims to be biblical? ◀

The apostles were dealing not with abstractions like poverty and wealth, but with poor people and rich people. "God takes people as they are. I discover that those people whom I marginalize, God takes up. The same is true for putting categories on people."

In the biblical view, God is prejudiced in favor of those

whom the successful shove off to the margins of society, not because the oppressed are particularly righteous (they often are not), "but because God is righteous; not because being poor is honorable, but because being rich and exploitative or being poor and oppressed denies the essence of the covenant and thus of a righteous God. The covenant community was accountable to a God who had assumed the role of a righteous king. If the biblical record holds together a suffering people and a caring, righteous God, then God and Jesus work on the side of justice and righteousness. Concretely, God is at work on behalf of me and my fellow blacks, and of all others who are treated unfairly, as if they were a 'no people.'"

According to the biblical story, God judges people on the basis of the ways they relate to and treat those on the margins. The prophets of Israel condemned the proud and the cruel for their indifference to the poor, and Jesus had a notorious reputation for keeping company with undesirables. The apostles saw that God's word was especially at home among those on the margins of influence and power; they confessed that the God who says "I will destroy the wisdom of the wise" has "made foolish the wisdom of the world"; they saw power made perfect in weakness; they declared, against all expectation, that the Lord of all comes as a servant.

THE WORD FROM THE MARGINS

Recognizing God's preference for the margins is only a preliminary step in confessing faith in God. Yet it is an essential step and not an easy one, since all of us who are "doing very well, thank you" like to consider ourselves God's special friends. Still, it is only a first step. What may be even harder is to listen to what those on the margins have to say about God. It is not likely to be what we like to hear, and we have a well-stocked arsenal of defense mechanisms to ward off the sharp things they may say.

Those blacks and those of other minorities who are pushed to the margins of American society know the realities about which the Bible speaks. Oppression and poverty are not categories of sociology for them: when the pharaoh oppressed the Hebrews, he had his foot on their necks; when the Gospel of Luke talks about the poor, it is not talking about an abstract "condition of poverty," but about poor people. And when the Bible talks about liberation, it is not talking about some vague spiritual freedom, but about people being let go from bondage, from being held as outcasts or on the outer edge of society, sometimes without even a platform from which a cry of protest can be heard. Those on the margins have a special capacity to discern the core meaning of the Bible because the questions that come naturally to them are indeed biblical questions.

What is said from the margins (God's center) to those of us in the center (God's margin)?

▶ My parents instilled in me a love of the church and made me realize that although most white Christians lived contradictory lives, we should not hate them. I was bothered by the question of why we blacks had a "place" and why whites were so mean. Somehow it came through that God was not what whites confessed by their lives, but rather a God of justice. ◀

▶ The memory of tradition which comes out of the biblical text helps us blacks a great deal; it gives us hope. We see evil doomed in the Red Sea. While blacks don't want to see white people drowned in the sea, there is a sense of excitement when the story is told! ◀

▶ In my early life I had to deal with racism at its height. Those who denied us because we were black also confessed God every Sunday. The problem is, what kind of God is being served? ◀

▶ My father, a minister for fifty years, held a Doctor of Divinity degree, and my mother graduated from a school of pharmacy; so both parents were "doctors." I have a Ph.D. Whites would ask, "Why aren't all blacks like you?" As I grew up I wondered, "Who is God? Why is God out to get me?" I could see nothing of the God of love, beauty, or justice of whom my father spoke every Sunday and of whom my mother, the church organist, played and sang. Evil confronted me at two points: being black in America, and having a speech impediment. How can I confess God? I am forced to see God as one who requires that we muddle through—it is our duty to do at least that. ◀

▶ Wardens in jail really understand black theology and fear it. Men are hungry for Scripture, for prayer, and for liberation. Black theology can make a tremendous difference to men in prisons and on drugs. Chaplains generally fear black theology because they fear the prisoners. They rarely speak to the prisoners as equals, but always with mistrust and fear that something is wrong with people behind bars. ◀

▶ Dehumanizing work, living conditions, or personal relations throttle the spirit, but do not condemn the spirit to terminal sickness. *Women of Crisis* by Robert and Jane Coles draws stunning portraits of women in tough cir-

cumstances who are both shrewdly reflective and prayerful. The migrant worker, the hotel maid, the supermarket
checker maintain a wisdom search, a spiritual life. ◀

For people on the margins, the problem of theology is
not to figure out "whether we in the modern world can
meaningfully talk about God," but "to see how things fit
under the sovereignty of God."

▶ The irony of birth is that it immediately poses the threat
of death. Polluted air, polluted water, polluted institutions, polluted individuals contribute to our death. Pride
of sex, pride of power, pride of race, pride of class, pride of
ideology bolster our demise. The pollution and pride point
to a propensity of human beings to cheapen life. This
cheapening process relates to a loss or an ignoring of the
sovereignty of God. Without this sense of awe, reverence,
mystery, holiness, and fear of God, idolatry becomes ram-
pant. Pride and pollution are merely symptomatic of a loss
of that consciousness of God. To put it briefly: A loss of the
sovereignty of God equals pride plus pollution, and ultimately death. ◀

Those on the margins sometimes take a long time to
break through the dividing walls others so carefully maintain to keep them at a distance. How many times have we
passed by "the man on the corner"?

▶ On a fine winter day he wears a stocking cap pulled
down over his ears. In summer you will see him in an old
suit coat. He stands on the corner, tape recorder in hand,
his voice goes on and on, his volume goes from a bare
whisper to a loud bellow. Even when his volume is in
midrange and you walk close by, it is difficult to under-

stand all the words. All the words, that is, except one. "God" always comes out at peak volume. You can hear that word a block away.

Hundreds of people hear that word as they rush from downtown offices to bus stop or parking lot. Two young office workers speculate as they rush by, "Maybe he's doing penance for some dastardly deed."

But hurry, your bus is coming! No time to hear him out. Let's go. You run for the bus, "God" firmly ringing in your ears.

A lot of questions go unanswered when you rush past the man on the corner, but you are certain of one thing: that man on the corner has some kind of a relationship with God. The second or third time you rush past, you notice that he doesn't have a box on the sidewalk and there is no upturned hat in his hand. You suddenly realize that this guy is for real. Secretly you feel proud that the old home town has a person like this. You don't make any more quips about him.

You realize that whatever his regular work, here is a man of God—in wrinkled old clothes. Maybe it's the sixth or seventh time you hear him when it suddenly hits you: he has more guts than I have. I sit in a comfortable church among friends and confess my faith in God. This guy gets out here in enemy territory and cuts loose, no matter who laughs at him, no matter what taunts are flung at him.

It seems that some people don't walk as fast past his corner as they once did. Maybe someday someone will even pause to listen to what he has to say.

By the way, you should know that the man on the corner is black, in case that makes any difference. ◀

Whatever the real reason might be, the reason we would give for rushing off would go something like this: "How can he be so sure he's right? Sure, he can express his views if he wants to; it's a free country, isn't it? But everybody is entitled to their opinion. His and mine just don't happen to be the same." We resist the claim that the marginalized may have a better understanding of God not only because the claim takes us off our pedestal, but also because we suspect that everything is a matter of interpretation, and we know everybody is going to look at things from a particular perspective. This sounds nobly tolerant, but it is in fact basically selfish because it means the only time we get indignant is when somebody strays onto what we think is our turf. "I'm happy for you to interpret the gospel any way you want—as long as it doesn't bother me."

RACISM AND SEXISM

In American society, white people, and especially the males, have had generations of practice at being in charge, and domination has become a habit. Today two groups are particularly vocal in their challenge to such domination. Other groups are on the margins with voices that are increasingly insistent. However, the challenge of blacks to American racism and of women to American sexism and, in particular, to racism and sexism in the churches, cannot be evaded by anyone concerned with faith in God today. Blacks and women say: "The biblical witness is clear; the problem is that racists and sexists claim to be the rightful authorities in interpreting God's word for all the rest of us. They accuse black power and women's liberation of being ideological, while it is the status quo that in fact exhibits the pathology of power and domination."

Among the signs of God's grace to the churches in America today are the blacks and women who are making the challenge from within the churches. They are committed to reconciliation so deeply and strongly that they stomach the abuse and misunderstanding and rage of those who deny them full liberation. These blacks and women are caught in a tension between their Christian identity and their racial or sexual identity. Christians denounce them for rending the body of Christ, and other blacks or women denounce them for selling out to an institution which reinforces oppression in the name of religion. Not to hear what the blacks and women are confessing in and to the churches is a denial of the gospel. Even at a practical, strategic level, not to pay attention to them is an act of folly.

The black Christian experience in our time is one in which the dynamic interplay of public worship and social action is more immediately apparent than in almost all predominantly white churches. "The prophetic critique of society in the black churches simply assumes celebration and praise of God." "I have a deep concern to understand God. It was begun in the black church. I knew something of black power long before the 1960s. It was in the church that the real things happened, like solidarity at the time of death. This led me to the social character of God."

While this connection between worship and action is very strong in the black experience, there are warnings that maintaining the connection requires steady attention.

▶ There is a need to recover a profound spirituality in the black religious tradition and, at the same time, to hold on to political, social, and economic radicalism. We have had a breakthrough on religion facing the real issues, but we have not cultivated the spirituality for this activism. The Western inability to perceive political life and personal life as a whole infects the black experience too. The merging of spirituality and radicalism marks a turning point in my

life, a point made terribly sharp by the death of my only
son in an automobile accident. ◄

Indeed, the problems for the blacks in confronting their
confession of faith in God are staggering. "Black suffering
derived from racism comes in a new form today: neo-
conservatism, privatism, stress on rugged individualism,
reactions against affirmative action and against the earlier
stress on minority rights, tax rebellions, unemployment,
underemployment, and so on. This web of suffering
catches not only blacks, but also those others on the bottom
who already suffer in good times. They all will be even
more maligned during hard times." "'Take this whole
world and give me Jesus' is not my kind of song. I want
a part of the world." "The white community is more
threatened by self-assurance on our side than by anything
else. In our suffering, God has been with us. The white
community has not suffered. We have survived with some
sense of destiny."

The oppression of women has been of a different sort—
less overt, more subtle. For many blacks, resources of
faith come from the core experience of the church as community. For most women, such resources must come from
elsewhere since the church community has mirrored
and frequently encouraged the societal subordination of
women.

▶ The human condition has become both the medium of
and the obstacle to my confession of faith. Before coming to
consciousness about the condition of women in the Roman
Catholic Church, I was an institutional Christian. What the
official church said was credible, necessary, and norma-
tive: the essential mediator of God's love and will for me.
Now, it is still the human church that reflects the divine
love for me, but in the negative: God has finally become

bigger than the church. God is mother as well as father. God has created me equal to the male. And God will deliver me and liberate me from the church's sin against creation. Institutionally, of course, women are denied the sacraments unless they are willing to participate when, how, and where men say they are permitted.

Yet through it all and certainly because of it all, I have come to know the crucified Christ. I have come to identify with the social gospel of the blacks. I have come to realize that only God is God. ◄

► Women are a majority pushed to the margins. If confessing faith in God is to deal with the real world, it will have to be persuasively countercultural on the question of women's rights, dignity, and potential contributions. To be full good news, the confession must provoke the male minority to rethink and reverse their treatment of the female majority.

To a culture and church that often do not want women's gifts, we women say, "Repent and believe in the good news that your majority party does have a great store of gifts, without which the nation and the church are sadly diminished." Despite civic laws or passionate theologies of equality, civic and religious institutions do not treat women as men's equals, do not give them equal access to responsibility, leadership, or financial and social rewards. From this situation women have developed the gift of a special, patient receptivity toward the God who offers a justice they don't find much of in time. Lately, however, women have been developing an anger often quite holy, and such anger too should be considered a gift to the church.

Both the lack of dignity and the anger may become sharper if I tie them to the troublesome question of sexist language. The question is parallel to white language about blacks. If a black person asks me to call her black instead of Negro, and I do not honor that request, I assault that black person's dignity. If a woman tells me that sexist language —for example, the generic "man" or "he"—offends her, or makes her somehow a second-rank possessor of human nature that men have in the first rank, and I refuse to honor what she says, I assault that woman's dignity. In the name of my literary style or my settled language habits or whatever, I say I will not take that woman seriously enough to stop hurting her. My conviction that language is an inconsequential matter or at least "nothing to get upset about" bulks larger than her self-revelation that she feels diminished or marginalized. Doesn't Christian faith urge us to cast off such selfish ways that hurt other people? You can't love your neighbor as yourself very impressively if you qualify this command whenever the neighbor is female.

So too with the question of language about God. There is a feminine imagery about God available in Scripture and a solid theological tradition that God is beyond gender (and so God is equally female and male). But our imaging God as mother the way we image God as father has not worked out. Indeed, there is clear derogatory feminine imagery in Scripture, such as the prophetic strand that calls Israel's infidelity harlotry and defilement.

Just as we deal with biblical treatments of slavery, so should we deal with those about women: bring it up to the more enlightened, more mature, more just conscience that contemporary times experience. And if we are serious about promoting women's dignity and equality, we will take some initiative in feminizing God, without being dragged kicking and screaming from our traditional imagery and language which says implicitly that God is male. We will write our speeches and compose our prayers with an evenhanded distribution of pronouns and images because we really believe this underappreciated group needs to have their natures placed in God too.

For what women do I speak? I believe I speak for all women, at least potentially. Simply by being a person of mind and heart, a woman wants justice, love, dignity. Of course the women's movement has imperfections which ought to be criticized. But those women who write off the core aims of feminism do so most ambiguously. Like blacks who identify with the white establishment or Jews who downplay the threat of anti-Semitism, these women are oppressed people trying to make it in an oppressor's world. The oppression of women clearly runs a wide range of seriousness, but any interpreter who reads women's resistance to women's core liberation as a vote for patriarchy or a vote for branding women's liberation trivial, is a fool. Freud had such difficulty finding out what women wanted because he didn't see them as human beings equal in dignity to himself. There is no mystery about what women want: to be neighbors, loved as you would love yourself.

I don't want to run into reverse sexism by stereotyping men. I have spoken of what I see and experience here and now: women's dignity is abused, their input undervalued. But my full church is bisexual, inclusive, as is my God. I want both men and women in community, heightened in their individuality by their relation to one another. By the way, that seems to me highly feminist. Community is a women's specialty. ◄

"ISN'T EVERYBODY MARGINALIZED?"

We squirm as the message of God on the margins comes clearer and clearer and our defenses become weaker and weaker. But don't we have a fallback position? Yes: "Isn't everybody marginalized?"

There is one overwhelming sense in which "all are marginalized" is profoundly, anxiously true.

▶ All of us surely share the feeling that the future is not what it was prior to 1945. We are now, all of us everywhere, a bomb culture. There are tremendous inequities on the earth, but we are all equal as we huddle under the bomb's shadow. In the week I write this, there have been two false alarms through a computer malfunction that have sent our strategic nuclear bombers into readiness alert just short of taking off.

What does this dread produce in us? It removes our sense of continuity. What will the future of my children or grandchildren be? Will they have life at all?

Yes, we who worship in most of the churches of the land are middle class, with a host of securities missing from the lives of those on the brink of survival all around the world and in our midst. Our shared dilemma today, however, is living in the nuclear age. I think it must preoccupy most Americans, whether the awareness is conscious or subconscious. How can human beings live creatively without a sense of continuity? ◀

The bomb does indeed create a kind of equality, a universal marginalization in which decisions a handful of people might make within less than an hour could literally push the entire human race beyond the margins of existence itself. We might have hoped that in the face of nuclear threat we would have been converted to a new awareness of the sinfulness of all our marginalizing, but that has not happened. We have in fact become ever more insistent on our right to nuclear superiority. With horrendous irony, we increasingly marginalize the rest of the world, oblivious to the fact that nuclear holocaust will be quite indifferent to national, racial, religious, and any other distinctions between us and them. "Every attempt to put America first pushes others away and behind into the margins where their very lives are not allowed to count as much as fluctuations in our standard of living. Our nation is in some ways institutionally committed to the marginalizing of others and to that extent is systematically opposed to the gospel, for all the pretense of 'In God We Trust.'"

The danger in asking, "Isn't everybody marginalized?" is that if everybody is on the margins, then nobody finally makes any real claims on our faith at all. If "all are marginalized" is not an adequate response to the news that God is on the margins, what sort of response is called for by those of us who are not on the margins?

LISTENING AND ACTING

First, we must listen. One person read one of our inquiry's interim reports and responded, "When I finished I thought that although it is good for people to come together to reflect on the confession of faith in God, I at this time would have very little to say in this group because I experience such an active presence of God where the poor of the world are reaching out to claim what is theirs. . . . I am not sure there is any confession of faith today apart from the oppression of people. . . . I felt lonely when I finished the paper, but only for a few minutes." Her feeling of loneliness directly challenges the rest of us; the fact that it lasted only a few minutes may mean that she did understand the gropings of some "reflective" types of people toward a confession of faith that will be as authentic as hers.

Second, we can admit that the real point of the challenge is not that we are called upon to indulge in a secretly gratifying display of middle-class guilt feelings, but rather that we must get clear about the gospel's call for our response. "The dilemma becomes: if I believe that salvation and confession have serious social dimensions but don't know how to respond, what does that mean for my own spiritual authenticity, integrity, or development?"

▶ I sit down with a statement by blacks. It mentions subtle institutionalized racism, criticizes specialists who don't confess outside the limits of their specialisms, and warns against talk that drifts toward abstractions and away from living folk. And of course here I am, attached to institutions, specialisms, and abstractions.

If now I quicken to the statement's eloquence, what do I do? Well, I go to my concrete bunker and write a paper on "Institutionalized Racism," which may be read by as many as nine other white professors. My mode of living took years to make a set of habits, some selfish and respectable. Short of a bloody and all-leveling cultural revolution, what power stands a chance of loosening the grip of those habits and making me more available as a basic, mobile human instead of a bunker dweller? By any common measure, after all, I'm one of the lucky ones.

The only thing that could change me is the watcher who reminds me that being one of the lucky ones is a very ambiguous position and, if I identify with that piece of luck, fatal; a watcher who asks, "What's the most important thing about you?" and if I answer, "My wonderful run of luck," turns away; or "What's the worst thing that could happen to you?" and if I answer, "My luck might run out," turns away. ◀

Third, we can work to have our churches give more support to faith's involvement with the marginalized and less support to our own powerful preference for a faith that relates us to God directly, without any annoying detours to and through the margins. "There is not enough support in the church to keep on being urgent." For some Christians, worship itself provides the support to "keep on being urgent."

▶ Church worship can make real my solidarity with the poor, the hungry, the oppressed, without becoming a secular political platform. Worship expresses the unity of the body of Christ, the unity of all God's children, and reminds us affluent members of those who are suffering. Paul accuses the well-fed Christians of Corinth of defiling the meaning of Eucharist because they neglect their hungry brothers and sisters. Eleven o'clock Sunday morning may still be the most segregated hour in America; that is an indictment of the churches. Worship should overflow into action for justice. ◀

For other Christians, the overflow from traditional worship is not enough support to "keep on being urgent." They find such support where a more direct demand is made.

▶ In the biblical story, we learn that doing God's will for society is working among the poor and the outcasts to empower them to achieve fully human conditions of life (and recognizing that God is particularly active in movements among the poor), and working among the rich and powerful to destroy their idolatries and enable them to become fully human.

I want constantly to escape this involvement because of what it requires of me. Quakerism has served my witnessing confession by accepting me only after I have shown a willingness to participate in the kingdom, thus making such confession absolutely central. I make this radical step not because I believe that I belong with muscular Christians, but because I am an ineffective leaven and witness without a strong community. ◀

Fourth, we can expect growth and change to follow our involvements. One does learn things by doing them, and there is a wealth of experience in past and present Christian tradition to show that practical ministry to the poor and oppressed has an overflow of meaning that itself becomes a source for new ventures in faith. What we can't imagine doing today can, with a little practice, become almost second nature tomorrow. "We find we are able to see Christ in others and in some instances discover we are more capable of unconditional love than we had thought." But here as in so many other places we can easily fool ourselves.

▶ When we catch ourselves marginalizing the poor, blacks, women, and begin to judge ourselves for doing so, we take steps of appropriate repentance. Then we start feeling better. And that just proves how hard we are to redeem: for these are just a few of our sins, and there are many more which we have scarcely begun to notice. What about our attitudes to and our treatment of those we think ugly, boorish, stupid, incompetent? How much do we do to help compensate for and correct the disadvantages that constantly burden the feeble or the timid or the emotionally confused or children? Justice's agenda is always terribly overloaded, much more than we notice. Our unfairness is vastly greater than we think. Love has inexhaustible work to do before we even have a good general beginning. ◀

Fifth, and most fundamentally, we can get straight about where the biblical questions are directed.

▶ * "Remember, those who have been placed on the mar-
    gin are in God's center."
  * "Blessed are you poor, for yours is the kingdom of
    God" (Luke 6:20).
  * "One does not live by bread alone" (Deut. 8:3 quoted
    in Matt. 4:4).

In authentic confession, who says these things to whom?

Does the wealthy person say them to the physically poor,
or to him or herself?

Does the well-fed say them to the hungry, or . . . ?

Does the literate say them to the illiterate, or . . . ?

Does the power-wielding male say them to the disen-
franchised female, or . . . ?

Does the happily married say them to the divorced-by-
rejection, or . . . ?

Does the athlete say them to the crippled, or . . . ?

In authentic confession, the wealthy, well-fed, and
others say these things to themselves. Then the confession bites, embarrassingly and painfully, and becomes
a call to surrender whatever within oneself (for example,
attitudes, motivations) or of oneself (for example, wealth,
power) is doing the marginalizing. Otherwise, what
could be authentic confession remains pernicious, trivial gossip.

And it becomes self-justifying, counter-gospel, ba-
nalized gossip if to others and to oneself the language
becomes spiritualized: "spiritual poverty," "crippled
souls," "wisdom of the uneducated," "power of power-
lessness," and so forth. Behind such gossip is usually a
filing cabinet way of looking at people. "Poor," "women,"
"the divorced" are reduced to classes and sets of numbers,
and someone begins to have demonic power over living
persons.

In short, confession about marginalization which does
not come from a contrite heart becomes irresponsible talk,

no matter what intellectual cohesion and relevant biblical information may flutter through it. ◀

▶ The test of such a contrite heart is the confessor's peaceful yet firm movement toward action. Love is shown in deeds. If we are sincere in following Jesus, we will make God's justice our habitual mind-set. We will vote, spend our time, spend our money, raise our voices to help the marginalized receive a fair share of the world's goods. There is no authentic confessing of faith in God that rests content with laws, systems, or ideologies that cast some human beings into semihumanity. Authentic confession does not act as though any people have the right to superfluities as long as any people lack necessities. Christian discipleship is more than action, but it cannot be anything less. ◀

7
Discovering Treasure

▶ Voices say that Bible and church are not persuasive. I want to listen to those voices. Problems in authenticity and authority can be fenced off, dodged, stonewalled; they can be put to sleep by ingenuity, by rhetoric, by piety. But when they awaken or break through, even if it takes centuries, they can cut deeply. I had lived happily with inerrant Scripture and infallible tradition. But for me such absolutes now are gone. How shall I confess the God they proclaimed? And if I can find a way, is it good to do so? ◀

Some Christians who know well the tradition are persuaded that "what we have inherited is not adequate to our present needs." Others also well versed in the tradition are unsure what role Scripture and church tradition play in our experience of confessing faith in God. "Neither Scripture nor church is why I believe. At least I don't think so. But then what can I say? My earliest impressions of God are rooted in both Scripture and the church. Without them, would I have come to belief at all?" Still others find they dare not judge whether the inheritance is adequate or not because they do not know what we have inherited. "My knowledge of the Bible, on a scale of one to ten would be minus six."

The past turns out to be both trap and treasure, and the trick is to avoid the trap and discover the treasure. While this dilemma is inescapable for any one or any group

125

conscious of living within a tradition, the dilemma has a special point for us today. For many centuries in the West, people did not have to make a choice to live within or outside the Christian tradition. For us, living in a highly pluralist age, the Christian tradition is an intentional choice among a bewildering variety of religious traditions, even explicitly non-religious ones.

The discovery of the treasure of the past is something many Christians recognize as part of confessing faith in God, but they are unsure how to make the discovery. "I want to think my values are based on my Christian faith, but when I try to reevaluate this I don't know how much I actually turn to faith and the Bible. I'm just not sure."

THE BURDEN AND BLESSING
OF THE PAST

What are we to do with the burden and blessing of the past? If the God we confess on the basis of the Bible is a God who "makes all things new," then why get buried under old documents and submit ourselves in any way to the authority of people long since dead?

To shout about the authority of Scripture and tradition, to insist that they (or only one of the two) contain everything that is authoritative and that everything they contain is authoritative, has overtones of fear that the Bible and the church cannot make their mark without our strident defense. "A church sexton found the minister's sermon notes on the pulpit and noticed in the margin, 'Point weak here—yell like hell!'"

A careful and considered use of the past is not easy to achieve, because of the drastic ignorance of the Bible and Christian tradition in the churches today. A church member who says, "Biblical background is clearly lacking in my life," speaks for multitudes and confirms what many surveys have shown: the Bible is as little read as it is much honored.

▶ Many people, if asked what the Bible means to them, would refer to Psalm 23 ("The Lord is my shepherd"), the Lord's Prayer, and John 3:16 ("God so loved the world") as the passages that help us best relate to God. This suggests a reliance on the verses that were learned by heart in Sunday school. You could certainly do worse than those in catching a vision of God, but there is so much more—in fact, so much that you might not be able to swallow the person of God in all the ways the Bible presents. But it's worth knowing what the Bible offers before you decide you can't get it down your throat. ◀

Ignorance is only the first hurdle to be cleared. The next hurdle looms when we know what the tradition is.

"Everybody has to call on a tradition. I find that calling on the biblical tradition raises a catalog of problems." The list begins with the difficulty we have understanding much of the Bible's language; extends through our suspecting the motives of those who at various times and places decided that these particular books, and not the many others also available, would be honored as uniquely authoritative; and finally focuses on those parts wherein God is portrayed not only as "not our kind of folks," but even as a kind of folks we couldn't admire or imitate, much less worship.

▶ Our church study group identified strongly with "God is not our kind of folks." But "What kind of folks is God?" will not be resolved by more reference to the authority of Scripture. That authority is not to be assumed. Even if study of the Bible conclusively proves a particular point, it lacks the power to direct church people.

Theologians and clergy may conclude this only shows lack of faith and obedience among the laity. But many lay people are questioning biblical authority for other reasons: (1) On certain points a consensus of biblical witness does agree, and laity still are unwilling to conform, at least in part because the clergy and theological community are also unwilling. Most commonly mentioned is the injunction in Luke 18:22 to "sell all you have and give to the poor." All agree the Bible says this and all agree no one is doing it. (2) A surprisingly sophisticated position emerges among the laity which emphasizes the dynamic rather than static nature of the Word. From this point of view, the Word is always becoming and thus is to be found today not only in the literal biblical witness. ◀

If one were to acknowledge Scripture alone as a guide of life, one would be in a quandary.

▶ If I had only Scripture as a source of guidance, I would have extraordinary difficulty determining central concerns: is slavery in accord with the gospel? Is civil disobedience ever justifiable? Should women have equal rights with men in secular or religious spheres? Should opposition to war and nuclear power and support of civil rights be major elements of my struggle for the kingdom of God? Or since Matt. 26:11 asserts that the poor will always be with me, and the Book of Revelation that Armageddon alone will stifle the reigning demonic powers in the world, should I not focus my energies on getting as many people as I can in all cultures to experience Jesus Christ as the Lord and Savior?

"Scripture alone" usually means "my interpretation of Scripture in light of my experience and convictions." I prefer to have that experience and conviction guided by the tradition (or, at least, *a* tradition)—certainly church tradition, but on occasion a nonchurch tradition. Consider the struggles against slavery and anti-Semitism, and for women's rights. From some scriptural texts, supporters of slavery clearly had the better argument, but the conscience of the church, gradually seeing the nature of slavery and experiencing its effects, developed over the course of a century a universal tradition which condemns slavery. Likewise with women's rights. And only very recently have Christians begun to be honest about the role of Christian theology and catechetics in encouraging and inflaming anti-Semitism.

But I am not happy talking about just Scripture and church tradition as sole authorities. There was a time when only a few prophets in the church spoke on behalf of abolition, women's rights, and the continuing legitimacy of Judaism in the total story of God's people. So one has to speak of Scripture, tradition, and Spirit-led conscience as the proper authorities. In the case of abolition and women's rights, the tutor which awakened conscience was a secular tradition—the same pressure for human rights that had led to the French and American Revolutions. It is a sign of the terrible dangers lurking in "Scripture and tradition alone" that only when Christians are confronted with the unimaginable horrors of the Holocaust do we reexamine biblical thought and Christian tradition about the Jewish people, past and present. ◀

THE INHERITANCE OF QUESTIONS

Calling on biblical and church tradition does indeed have a catalog of problems. To deal effectively with the problems, we need to clear up misunderstandings and try different ways of relating to the past. The inheritance is not only of answers, some of which we probably want to reject, but also of questions which we would probably like to avoid, so they must be asked repeatedly.

▶ So many questions people have about the Bible are the questions of the Bible. "It would be easier to understand the problem of evil from a materialistic, agnostic perspective where one might simply say there is no reason or plan; things just happen." That's just the point—it would be easier. The Bible makes things harder. If the Bible offers an answer to the problem of evil, it does so only after unflinchingly posing and facing the problem. ◀

Does the authority of the Bible reside exactly at the level of questions? The questions of the Bible are the same as our own, but the answers given for any historic moment may be vastly different.

▶ Do we speak of the "truth" of Scripture? I prefer the term "reality." Sin is real, salvation is real. Truth as a category doesn't arise, at least not often, in the Bible. The real is more prominent. We cannot approach the text with objectivity. The text has a lot of life and vitality of its own. We are engaged in a dialogue with the text. Is the text true, that is, does it conform to reality? What does it mean to me? The response comes in dialogue with the text. Frequently, as in Job or in the parables of Jesus. the response which comes from the text is a series of questions. ◀

When the past proves to be a trap, it is often a trap of our own devising. We may indulge in nostalgia for a "good old days" that never existed, failing to realize that the past was every bit as incomplete and unclear, as full of promise and peril, as our today. "The past is in some respects deceptive. It suggests that traditional modes of confession are adequate." But the deception is not wholly in the past; we also deceive ourselves by pinning past confessors of faith to a board, as though they were specimens in a natural history museum. We treat the bearers of tradition as static authorities, and so we have our guard up (because we always have our guard up when we are in the presence of authorities). If, however, we approach persons of the past to learn from their way of confessing faith in God in their today something of use for our confessing in our today, their authority comes from their confession; and their confession invites us, not imposes upon us. The past need not stifle faith. It can help awaken faith.

"CONFESS AS WE CONFESSED"

Many from the past whose voices Christians regard as authoritative were themselves critical of the tradition they had inherited. It is our problem, not the past's, if we insist on making the past say, "Confess *what* we confessed in exactly the same terms with the same understandings." The problem is still ours, but it is the right kind of problem if we listen to the past saying, "Confess *as* we confessed; know and serve the God to whom our confession pointed in our time and to whom your confession must point in your time."

These problems are not new, and the church has not had to wait until the late twentieth century to hear some radical solutions. A third-century Christian wrote, "The Scripture interwove in the history some events that did not take place, sometimes what could not have happened; sometimes what could but did not . . . in order that [readers might learn how] a meaning worthy of God must be sought out" (Origen, *On First Principles*, IV.i.15). Origen's admission that the Bible is made up of different kinds of statements does not, of course, solve the problems that the different kinds of statements present to interpreters, but it does locate responsibility where it belongs: on the Christian believer to make distinctions and search out "a meaning worthy of God."

The past is a strange, peculiar treasure. It's like those close friends we truly value who always tell us what they really think, even though much of the time we'd rather be with more distant people who tell us what we want to hear.

▶ We shortchange ourselves when we look to the past only for what we judge to be relevant to us right now. The very "strangeness" of the past is one of its positive features. God, by choosing history as the arena of revelation, comes to us in ways that do not always speak directly to our condition, except by alerting us to the fact that our condition is probably not what we thought it was and almost certainly not what we would like to think it is. The past is, of course, subject to interpretation, but we cannot make it over entirely in our own image. ◀

"Scripture opens up various traditions of the history of God's people and thus helps keep me from making my own tradition the only true one. The one thing which stands out, however, is that the God of all the Old and the New Testament traditions is the same God." In terms of what forms us spiritually, most American Christians are quite untouched by the Old Testament. With its provocative deposit of social consciousness, it slides into the background. In shaping our thought and feeling, such neglect is reinforced by treating the Old Testament either as entirely superseded by the New Testament or as a mere anticipation of the New Testament event. We thereby cheat ourselves of a major source of the knowledge of God.

▶ Scripture can decisively shape our confessing of God without our claiming Scripture alone as sufficient to supply all religious images and language. And this is precisely to honor biblical authority, because we enter into Scripture as into the memories of the various struggles of faith with unfaith. When we become engaged with the Bible's record of debate and encounter, and especially when we notice God's extraordinary recognition of our diverse ways of responding, we can be shocked into the deeper authority of Scripture. The Bible persuades us of its own authority. ◀

▶ There's an old story. A simple Christian listens to a professor's lecture on biblical problems such as form criticism, demythologizing, and hermeneutics, and then says, "It's not what I don't understand about the Bible that disturbs me; it's what I do understand." I used to think that story quaint, and in my way of hearing it, the professor came out on top. No more.

I now see that the issue is not "intellectual versus anti-intellectual," but rather "abstract versus personal." An abstract reading can be very unintelligent, though decked out in all sorts of professional finery. We set up a whole series of mufflers between ourselves and the text (it is ancient, mythological, patriarchal, and so on). We read and read, but do not hear the instruction the text has to offer.

I do not for a minute think the difficulties aren't there, but I am increasingly persuaded that we don't have to get all those questions figured out first before we can read the text properly. Indeed, the questions "How are the Scriptures inspired?" or "In what sense is the Bible revelation?" cannot be solved in advance of reading. The Bible plants in us skepticism about any theories of inspiration or revelation, for the Bible repeatedly demonstrates that when God has something to reveal, it is not what we would have expected. If the God of the Bible is to remain God, we cannot put a lock on the door of surprises. The proper prayer for anyone who wants to pick up the signals of revelation from the Bible is this: "Lord, teach me to be silent so I can hear you interrupting me." ◄

All of us participating in the Institute's inquiry group reported undergoing significant changes, ranging from mild tremors to seismic shocks. In the uncertainty caused by change, we went to sources of faith, particularly the Bible and close friends, and found there new possibilities for faith. In the process of personal change or as a result of the process, the Bible, especially the Old Testament, appeared new and fresh. The Bible was no longer a book at a distance, a series of problems to be solved, or a hindrance to be left behind. It provided ways of understanding the changes themselves.

► When teaching the Bible, I try to expose and interpret to students the mind of each of the authors of the biblical literature. This leads to the faith commitment of those authors and reveals the fact that I hardly begin to confess faith in these ways. In other words, teaching the Bible forces me to question the quality of my own witness. I am brought up against the stubborn fact that I simply do not know how to confess my own faith. ◄

Notice this response to the Bible. The problem is not: "This is an ancient text; these people lived in a culture very different from mine, so how can I extract anything from this old document that will be of use to me?" The problem is: "This puts me on the spot." Putting us on the spot is one of the ways the inheritance proves to be a treasure.

▶ What is the order of moves in the interpretation of Scripture: do we go to Scripture out of suffering and back to suffering, or do we start with the Bible, then move to the human situation of suffering, and return to the Bible? A black biblical scholar put it this way: "Scholars insist on the historical-critical method to get at the truth, and of course I use it. But in my experience there must be confession: I bring my own self in, in the confessional way. Then there must be the Scripture: let the Bible come back to you so that there is judgment upon you." Not only do we interpret the text; the text also interprets us. ◀

▶ The God of whom I speak is known in a revelatory experience via the Bible: a *creating* and *sustaining* God. God *elected* a covenantal people for special responsibility; *led* those people out of Egyptian slavery through perceived miracles and devastation of the "enemy" into the promised land of Canaan; *chastened, disciplined,* and *judged* the elected people when they failed to be true to the covenant and the codes of law as epitomized in Exodus and Deuteronomy; *acted* in strange ways when the chosen people failed to be true to their calling for special responsibility and opted for special privilege; *enabled* or *allowed* foreigners to execute the perceived will of God on a people who refused to see that justice and mercy are required toward the poor and marginals of society—not because the poor are so righteous, but because the covenant community was to be accountable to a God who had assumed the role of a righteous monarch: *exercised* grace not only by judging via the prophets, but also by enabling those same prophets to point toward forgiveness for a wayward people; *further provided grace* by sustaining the chosen people in exile, saving a remnant so as to allow for their return and the renewal of the faith; *protected* the people of

Israel when mightier countries devastated their land and yet *motivated* Israel to sing psalms, to reflect on the meaning of existence (the Writings), and to long for a time of political, religious, social, and economic peace (messianic age).

This same God sent Jesus, whom we confess through faith to be what the New Testament writers interpreted him to be. In the coming of Jesus, that messianic age promised in Old Testament history has dawned. In the life, teaching, ministry, death, and resurrection of Jesus, God's self-revelation happens in a unique way. Because of the resurrection, God has exalted Jesus to the right hand (power). The Holy Spirit's presence in the church makes Jesus Christ's presence felt and known today. Jesus is present with power today, but we expect his return with greater power when there is consummation of his will. We are to repent, believe, and be baptized. Jesus proclaimed the kingdom of God while we proclaim Jesus Christ. One need not be separated from the other if we understand that the kingdom of God has to do with God's reign in the lives of persons and nations, and that we have a foretaste and model of that reign in Jesus Christ.

Persons who were on the margins—who were in need and who expected a savior, someone who cared—heard and responded to Jesus' signs, deeds, and words. God, as proclaimed by Jesus, forgave sins, healed diseases, and set people free to feel good about themselves, empowered to live as free persons. Once people, whether marginal or mainstream, are energized with the knowledge of God, they are free to live and let live. Once I know to whom I belong, I can no longer tolerate the thwarting of anyone who seeks that knowledge, power, and freedom to become a child of God. In other words, the gospel sets me free to be for myself and for the other. God's action is seen in the past, but God's action is progressive; God's self-revelation occurs even today in wacky but real ways. ◄

THE INHERITANCE INTERPRETS US

The inheritance interprets and judges us; it will also aid us if we approach it not for definitive solutions, but rather as part of our confessing.

The past is a treasure because it gives us perspective on ourselves. It is a treasure also because it gives us perspective on the age in which we live.

To affirm a central church tradition is not to suggest that there is a core of Christian doctrine or practice to which we can point and against which particular traditions can be measured. In the ecumenical age, we are in a process of discovering the central church tradition.

In this process of discovery, Catholic, Orthodox, and Protestant churches join. Churches of the world throughout North, East, South, and West join. The central church tradition in one sense exists by faith and not yet by sight. Yet the process of ecumenical discovery and the faith in our oneness in the body of Christ are together the essential corrective needed by all of us.

From the central church tradition so understood, we in American culture, who are of course products of our own history, receive insight and encounter the experience of others in different times and cultures. As we search for what it means to confess faith in God, the central church tradition must be given conscious attention critically because we are conditioned by it and positively because we are inheritors of the wisdom to be gained from it.

The past, which can be a trap for us unless we are careful, can keep us from falling into the trap of the present. We cannot extract ourselves from where and when we are, but we need not assume that the possibilities open to us begin and end with the world immediately around us. We can become so obsessed with our plight as modern (or even postmodern) persons that we let the present control the agenda of our lives. We do not have to be entirely children of our own age. And if we can get some critical distance on our own time by means of the past, we may be spared the rush to judgment which declares the trivial or the merely current to be the decisive word on the possibility or impossibility of faith in God. Far from suggesting that inherited modes of confession are adequate for our time, the past suggests, on the contrary, that all modes of confessing faith in God are incomplete, whether they are the modes of a yesterday that was once a today or of a today that will soon be a yesterday or of a tomorrow that will soon be a today.

READING CONVERSATIONALLY

Experts can help us get critical distance. Biblical scholarship has achieved wonderful results of clarification and insight. It has also—not entirely intentionally—persuaded multitudes of Christians that without extensive scholarly equipment, you can't read the Bible in a responsible way. But professional expertise is not the main requirement. Confessional openness is.

▶ How to read the Bible nonprofessionally is the topic I warm to. My temptation is to ape the airs of professional readers—the Scripture scholar, theologian, professor of Near Eastern languages, and sometimes the process philosopher, phenomenologist, existentialist, and other producers of sonorous glosses. Attractive, too, are brainy-sounding questions such as "What is the meaning of revelation or inspiration?" So this is the record of someone trying to fight off a certain temptation.

Well-known problems about the authority, inspiration, and revelatory character of the Bible tend to lose their bite in the course of a conversational reading. One does not, as one reads, get proofs that the book has those sides to it, but the reading acts as a paint remover over a stretch of time, gradually dissolving away doubts that it has those sides. My doubts, which seemed deep and cerebral, turn out to be complicated kinds of balk.

The mistake we see most often in "professional" readers of the Bible is that they look for assurances of inspiration and authority first, or as a precondition for letting the thing confront them directly. What happens then? The texts go silent, like Christ before Pilate when asked, "What is truth?" For what if it goes the other way? What if an informal conversational interview with the texts is precisely what rinses away, smiles away, sometimes laughs away my doubts about such matters as inspiration and shows me that my demands for assurance on those matters were ways of postponing conversation?

That the Word of God is "living and active" is nowhere clearer than in its ability to clam up when a team of professional interrogators drags heavy equipment up to it and says, "We have ways of making you talk!" That approach, using all-out scholarly force, is just the opposite of conversation. Conversational reading does not presuppose scholarly acquisitions. It means reading the texts the way we read private letters, as distinct from those marked "Occupant." As we read, we need to be prepared to hold up our end of a conversation which arises naturally, not one which is prompted by theological or other matters. ◀

Approaching the text conversationally is not easy for us

to do because we are so used to having theological or other matters loom large.

▶ The priest in his homily on the story of Jesus' feeding the multitudes said something like this: "Maybe it didn't happen in just that way. Maybe the sight of that youngster full of the spontaneity of youth, offering to share his few pieces of bread with the great throng, prompted one after another to bring out a hidden supply of provisions and start sharing."

I began picturing all those people pushing bread, raisins, smoked mullet, and halvah at each other until the whole thing turned into a picnic with softball, three-legged races, bluegrass shofar, and the like, but this I'm sure was entirely out of order. Still, it was as if the priest, if not himself embarrassed by the miracle element in the text, was very much afraid that we in the pews would be, so he furnished us all with a set of contact lenses for softening the glare. What exactly was that kindly priest trying to protect me from? "Glare," of course, is only a figure of speech.

The priest was trying to protect my modern consciousness—we each have one of those, and it's wonderful—from being ravished and taken over by something called a biblical mentality. Forces were on the move trying to make me a 2000-year-old man or possibly a somewhat younger man with a mentality 2000 years behind the times.

Then this question: would I want a biblical mentality? In one respect it seems I would, at least in relation to incidents like feeding the multitudes or walking on water—those incidents that theologians of the Romantic Age called nature miracles.

We are told something about the biblical mentality through the witnesses' reactions to those incidents. Some people were turned on and some were turned off. In that respect the biblical mentality sounds pretty much like ours. I tried to imagine an onlooker, someone in the third row, hungry like everyone else but also very intent on what was happening. She watches closely as the bread is blessed, follows with her eyes as the disciples pass out bread endlessly from God knows where, and when it is over she stares at the twelve baskets of leftover pieces with one question on her mind: "Why the hell can't I do that?" Not "How is that phenomenon possible?" but "Why him and not me?"

This illustrates one feature of the biblical mentality that I want for myself. When there's glare, I want to be free to notice the glare. I don't want anybody slipping Polaroid lenses between me and the print. What if the glare itself has something to tell me? It started our imaginary onlooker on a quest to pin down the difference between herself and the one who fed the multitudes, and who knows what the quest will turn up?

For such reasons I would say to that priest: "Don't try to protect my eyes from the glare of that text. Maybe a loaf of bread more or less is no big deal, but think how many other ways of starving there are. Starving for company, for love, for a sense of being somebody, for peace, for forgiveness, even for I know not what. If Matthew wants to portray someone who's on top of human cravings and starvings, don't shield me from the dazzle of it. Don't smoke the glass and hide the difference." ◀

Our unfamiliarity with this sort of conversational reading of the Bible does not result only from our lack of biblical knowledge, but because we are not accustomed to talking at this level with others (or even with ourselves). So we have all the hesitations that go with entering strange territory.

▶ We have been taught that nothing can be understood

apart from its context. So I begin my listening by placing everyone, including myself, in context—Catholic, Protestant, Orthodox, female, male, academic, monk, young, old, radical, traditional, and so on.

As I begin really to listen, I discover that these contexts are more a barrier than a help to true understanding of what each one, including myself, is about. The context which clarifies is the world we create in conversation with each other. This new world of confessional life together becomes our context, which none of us could have anticipated or fashioned by our own manipulation. We begin to breathe a different air, feel a different wind.

From this new perspective, the old distinctions (contexts) don't disappear, but they become grace notes to our identity, not the melody itself.

We come to the Bible loaded with machinery for context construction. The text is ancient, mythological; we are modern persons. So we are on guard, our defenses are up. We are taught to expect the text to be difficult for us to understand.

If, however, we learn to listen or are caught off guard, we discover that the Bible is an invitation to enter a confessional world. When we start looking *with* the Bible instead of *at* it (like looking with each other and learning what the real context of our group is instead of at each other in terms of preformed contexts), we get into conversation with it, and unexpected possibilities emerge. This can be scary because we are not in control. If we get into conversation with Joshua, for instance, we do not let our skepticism about heavenly messengers shield us from the glare: God answers "No!" when asked, "Are you for us or for them?" That doctrine was as hard for the ancient Israelites as it is for us, even though they may have had fewer difficulties with reports of heavenly messenger sightings. ◀

READING TOGETHER

Discovery of the treasure that each of us can be to one another and of the treasure that the past can be for us happens in conversation, in communion, in community. One church group put the whole matter very simply and very profoundly: "We need to read the Bible with someone else." A community composed the Bible for a community, and while the Bible can serve to nourish private devotions, when it is so used it is really being treated "out of context." "I believe it is essential to reading the Word of God that it be done in the church; the stronger our sense of interdependence and the stronger our willingness to share the Word with one another, the more will we be living examples of the formative influence of the Word because the Word will in fact be forming our lives, especially our life together as the church." "I have come to know that my experience is terribly partial, and thus I must guard against the temptation to let my individual experience 'control' the message in the tradition."

Learning to read together is an essential part of learning to be the pilgrim people of God, and being part of that people, in the fullness of its corporate life, is an essential part of learning to read.

▶ I accept the salvational character of the Bible, but distrust any pretense that I can discover the saving thread without the guidance of the church today as it (1) teaches in official words, (2) prays in its sacramental liturgies, and (3) "does the truth in charity," principally through the "little ones" in the church in the midst of their own suffering.

I must bear the tension between my belief that the community of the faithful as a whole, as the body of the risen Christ, is graced by God in such an infallible way that

God's most basic saving purposes for the church—doing, teaching, praying—can never be set completely awry by the likes of us, and my belief and experience that this same community can also be fallible—and too often is—and sinful in specific acts.

What has eroded from the central church tradition can be discerned only by rereading the Scriptures and the traditions through the prisms of the poor, that is, the marginalized, especially those whose lives are completely determined by the decisions of those at the top of the pyramid. ◄

There are many ways in which we can learn to read together. The most effective is one that is ready at hand, but is seldom recognized as a means of recovery and discovery of the treasure of the past: worship. We too often think of worship as something we plan, something we are in charge of. On occasion, though, it takes charge of us.

Forms of Christian worship vary, but common to nearly all of them are one or more elements of remembering: Scripture readings, psalms, ancient prayers, traditional creeds, celebration of the Eucharist. These forms, which can periodically become dry bones that need to be brought to life again, are the stuff of a common memory. Rightly employed, they remind us that the pilgrim people among whom we live and move and have our being are not simply those who are alive today. The history of the people of God (by no means a uniformly pretty history) is our history, is ourselves.

► I want to claim continuity with the body of Christians who have gone before me, who have safeguarded the treasure of the faith and have endured great persecution and hardship, and who have handed this treasure (this window into reality) on to me. I desire that my confession be the same as that of my sister and brother Christians. I also want it to be different. It is my confession in my age, my culture, my world view. If repeating an old formulation distorts the meaning of the reality I am confessing, I opt for the reality, not the formulation. ◄

The awakening of our common memory keeps alive in us the truth that the Exodus and the Day of Pentecost, as well as this morning's newspaper, are the story of our life.

8
Faith and What's Happening

▶ Charles and Gretchen told our church study group about the deep rift in their marriage caused by the Vietnam War, and how it had taken him a long time to agree with her immediate stand for peace and against U.S. involvement there. Charles said that now he can see more clearly where God is at work in the world issues of our times and lives.

Jim processed many issues of our lives under the theme of God's having left much of life for us to develop and create. Charles added that all of these areas raise questions that are for the best for us to face in maturing our faith. Sandra felt that crises had nourished her faith. Jim also said he knew many scientific types around the university who consider that the Christians too often define God in small terms and deal with insignificant issues, not the important ones. ◀

Why is it that we shy away from the big issues? Why do Christians these days shrink time and space, sometimes to a point where the only thought we give to God is in the tiny arena "God and me"? Why do we "neglect the dimension of God's purpose for humanity, for the peoples and nations within humanity, for the church within them all, and for each of us within God's great plan"? Why does it take a national trauma and a strain in his marriage to show Charles that God is at work?

Part of the reason is that powerful cultural forces have shaped us.

We have seen the emergence of a "me" culture—my growth, my self-development, my security, my self-interest, my well-being, and the rest. To what extent does our concern for our personal relation to God and our neglect of God's purpose for humanity as a whole reflect the "me" culture of contemporary America?

Perhaps we avoid trying to interpret the big picture because we are caught in the "me" culture. Or we could be caught in the "me" culture because the big picture is too baffling. Either way our convictions about God can be distorted. "Faith has little doubt that this world will end well and little knowledge of what this means." Or the much knowledge we already have causes that little doubt to grow and grow.

▶ Our study group included a couple whose child died because of a birth defect. How do we reconcile death, disability, the random chance of genetics and accident with the notion of God's power and care? We recall such biblical phrases as "the sun shall not smite you by day or the moon by night," "consider the lilies of the field," "the hairs of your head are numbered"—radical messages of a particular caring, sounding like protective watchfulness and loving concern by our Creator.

How can we be confident of a loving powerful God being with the origins and endings of the universe when we experience such vast impersonal forces which take no account of individuals and their needs? Tidal waves, earthquakes, famine, and starvation are difficult to relate to whether God knows, causes, or cares about what happens to persons. Why should the universe be designed in such a way that severe retardation and disability be a given for the lives of some people? It would be easier to understand from a materialistic agnostic perspective; one might simply respond that there is no reason or plan. Things just happen.

Some of the group were confident in creation as good and in the ultimate victory of good over evil, with a lot of struggle in between. Others wondered how to gain and keep such confidence in the face of tragedy that could not be directly attributed to human failures and downright sin. ◀

THE PROBLEM OF EVIL

This question is not new. Across the centuries, the problem of evil has been formulated in countless ways, and has generated a wide range of proposed answers. But every generation and every individual has to face it anew. Here, perhaps more than anywhere else, a confession of faith in God must be worked out personally; it just will not do to repeat somebody else's formula, though it is instructive to listen to what other people say in their words and in their actions. "We can think of Mother Teresa in Calcutta, Helder Camara in Brazil, Beyers Naudé in South Africa, and many a black Christian in the United States, who see more evil in a week than most of us do in a lifetime and who yet possess a powerful faith that is not eroded by the existence of evil." In other words, there are people who live out a practical theology somewhere between a "God and me" privatism and throwing up their hands in the face of the great crimes of history.

▶ No Christian can escape being profoundly troubled by evil. Why, however, does the problem of evil seem to nag at our minds and spirits? Is the problem of reconciling a good and powerful God with the existence of evil an intellectual problem for us? Or does the prominence of the problem mean that we are more in a state of groping than we are in a condition of being committed?

Many Christians accept the sentence, "Lord, forget what I call happy; make me what you call happy." But it is difficult to pray this with a certainty that takes away our fears of what might happen when the crunch comes. Is it because we are in the state of "Lord, I believe; help thou my unbelief," or because we want to give our lives over to God but are unable, that we do not really know the power of God to overcome evil, and so we allow the problem of evil to stand in our way?

I do not know the answer, but the question is as prominent among us today as that other troubling one—the place of Christ in confessing faith in God. God in Christ and God in history—the heart of our faith is, indeed, the nub of our puzzlement. ◄

HISTORY'S DIRECTION?

Christians are tongue-tied by the puzzlement about God and history. Some people, to be sure, have no doubts in another sense: God's purposes coincide with the interests of the United States, and since God is number one, the U.S. must be number one too. But other Christians, aware that God is not our kind of folks and that "the last will be first and the first last," are unwilling to identify our personal or national purposes with God's.

► I have lived a relatively calm personal life—nothing to shake me up much there. But the turmoil of world events —the Vietnam War, the assassinations of King and the Kennedys, the race riots—have led me to question how (or whether) God actually works in the world. I believe history is supposed to be moving toward something, but it is hard to see where the values lie or in which direction we are moving. ◀

▶ Most of us North American Christians have lost our vision of God's action in history. Our Christianity may continue to serve our private needs well enough to hatch, match, patch, and dispatch us, but there is much confusion about where the church is headed, little sense of urgency about where God is calling for action, little sense of dynamism and movement. We used to get our communal sense of participation in the sweep of salvation history by means of denominational vision or the church's home and foreign mission activity and the spread of Christian and Western influence or the conviction that the United States was a particularly chosen people. Now we have seen those sources of meaning for a public faith erode. ◀

We are tongue-tied at the very time when the world may be especially receptive to—even eager for—a word about God in history, spoken confidently by Christians.

▶ We cannot prove that our era is an important or extraordinary one in God's scheme, but it is the only era we have in which to confess faith in God. And, without being too shortsighted, we can detect signs that our times could be a critical turning point in human history which God may be providing for us. Communications now report the evils all over the world directly into our living rooms every night. Never before could people become so aware of the rest of the human family everywhere.

It is painful to accept and get used to this new situation. But what do we suppose God wants? The God in whom I believe has always wanted the whole human family to know one another, care about one another, protect and share in the riches of this lovely planet. We are the first people for whom this is possible. ◄

Can we loosen our tongues? If we can, do we have anything to say?

► The discussion moved along the lines of "How well is God handling current history?" I asked, "Whose problem is that?" I didn't think it was mine and was glad it wasn't. Maybe I shouldn't have asked since a few others claimed it was their problem. So we ended on a divided note. ◄

"God's handling of current history is not my problem" is not necessarily an offhand dismissal of a deeply disturbing question; it may indirectly focus attention where it should be. But first we must get clear why, for some Christians, "God's handling of current history" stands in the way of their confession of faith.

We ask: "How is God handling *my* history?" "I do not think of myself as one harshly suffering. And for a long time I was willing to believe that ultimate goodness coincides with our definition of goodness. But now the threat of my own death, soon to come as the result of a relentless disease, makes me assert, 'My own father wouldn't do this to me.'" "My cousin's death in an auto accident when we were still teenagers was a great blow to me. I couldn't understand how God could allow such things to happen. Later on, the college I had set my heart on turned down my application. I had prayed so hard for it, and I simply couldn't accept the results. My mother told me, 'Sometimes God's answer to a prayer is no, and in time you see things work out well in a different way.' Working through both experiences did strengthen my faith." Of course, there are people who could report that things worked out badly in a different way.

We also ask, "How is God handling the larger issues of history?" Comparisons and contrasts with the past are themselves full of problems since we may be very uneasy about claims made for past events.

▶ Some of the problems: (1) I don't see the grounds for saying that this event is God's work and that one isn't. (2) Many of the side effects seem unworthy—I like the rescue of the Israelites, but balk at the slaughter of dutiful Egyptian charioteers. (3) The values and causes supported by the supposed divine interventions seem to me rather narrowly provincial in most instances. (4) The overall results are not particularly impressive. (5) I find it morally impossible to reconcile myself with the proposition that God has withheld intervention in various instances of suffering and evil when there might have been effective intervention. In short, my sense of satisfaction, comfort, and appropriateness dissolves when I try to think more thoroughly about the traditional view of God's action in the world. The world no longer looks to me like one run by a God I want to confess.

I can appeal to mystery: God's ways are not mine. But I can't shake the feeling that if these are God's ways, they are not as good as they should be. I shudder at the audacity, and would recant and repent if persuaded that this is in fact the way it is. But from this feeling arises a grave doubt about whether this in fact could be the way it is. ◄

Expressions of puzzlement multiply. "I experience God as the One who will be there on the next day. What I need and want in my confessing is more of a sense of God in the present, of God today making my life and the world around

me new. I would like to live and dwell in that awareness of
the presence of God." "If I think of God as a remote rather
than a personal God, and if I believe God cannot be concerned with personal affairs, this uncertainty will lead to
my less witnessing to God's love." "A certainty: God's Son
was sent that we might see One who feels compassion,
who heals, who forgives, who restores. How then can God
allow so much misery in the world today?" "How easily we
forget the horror of the historical evil we have done in
God's name by transferring to God our own personal and
collective pathologies for divine sanction and approval.
We thus reveal our worst selves rather than confess the
true God."

EVIL AND SUFFERING FROM
THE RECEIVING END

All these questions are intensely real, but the particular
form in which they come is conditioned by the status of
those who ask them. The form most familiar to most of us is
determined by relatively well-off people. But do we listen
to the ways in which the questions about evil and suffering
are addressed by people who have been on the receiving
end of evil and suffering much more often and much longer
than so many of us? When black American Christians are
asked, "When you don't get justice, and everything goes
bad, where is God?" we presume the answer would be,
"Nowhere," or at best, "Absent." But that is not their
answer.

Suffering by blacks, of course, can be intensified by
anguish that knows no racial barriers.

▶ I began to look seriously at my life. "What will I be
able to do that will really matter? What primary projects
may I initiate and carry through in the period of active life
remaining?"

Then came my only son's death in an automobile accident. He was healthy, vigorous, on the eve of his adult-
hood. He had selected a vocation toward which he was
moving.

Out of this I have come to certain conclusions about faith
and my own suffering. Before this personal tragedy, I had
been mainly preoccupied with ethnic suffering—the suffering of black people. Now I had to ask, "Why did this
happen? What about God? What can I say to myself and my
family?"

I had a compulsion to give the eulogy at my son's funeral.
This required that I assess how God and faith inform my
life. Friends were a great support and one said to me, "If
you can understand what God is saying in this experience,
you will know more about what to do from now on." A
minister said to me at the graveside, "Thank you for your
confession of faith." I had not thought of it that way. ◄

A group of black Christians spoke of the question of
theodicy, traditionally defined as "justifying the ways of
God to humankind," and how that question haunts any
consideration of faith for black people. But black reflection
on the question seems to dig deeper and get further than
most traditional Christian thought. For a start, the question is defined in a fresh way, and the puzzle is located not
where those who are relatively comfortable put it (the
existence of evil), but where the marginalized experience it
(the persistence of evil).

► Theodicy is reflection upon human anguish against the
background of a belief in the goodness and power of God.
The justice of God in the face of the undeserved suffering of
the righteous is also implied. Blacks confront this problem
as persons and as a people. God is believed by Christians
to be a God of justice and omnipotence. Love is confessed

to be at the heart of God. Why does evil exist and persist? Why does a whole people suffer because of the way a benevolent Creator made them?

Any faith approach to theodicy must come to terms with mystery. There is much in the experience of suffering we may never fully understand. Sin as traditionally defined does not explain ethnic suffering. Black suffering is not completely explainable. The classical arguments may be reviewed, but they do not cast significant light on the problem. We can only expect to open up the issue a little.

Some suggested that theodicy may not be the problem with which blacks should be most concerned. Evil may not be easy to explain, but it is certain that God does not cause it. The evil that human beings can do something about is what really bothers us. We should attend to the business at hand.

The meaning of the resurrection is that we transmute evil into good. The real concern should be how we cope in a stressful situation. The important thing is what God requires us to do. The Bible says that evil does not destroy faith in God. We have testimonies that people have looked into meaninglessness and seen something beyond meaninglessness.

Theodicy is giving an explanation of evil in the light of prior affirmations about God. We can make certain affirmations in the face of suffering which make a great difference for our future. We can assert, even upon the loss of a loved one, that life has meaning because of what we believe about God. We need to distinguish between suffering and evil. Is all suffering evil? Suffering and evil are closely allied, but they can exist together or apart.

"Black students came to my classes in theology with the awareness of so much pain that I was driven to theodicy. Everything else crystallized around this. The questions are simply in the air. The students' experiences in relation to ideas about God gave birth to the questions. Theodicy assumes God is good and all powerful. Personal and corporate suffering intensifies the matter."

One member of the group said the very words everyone needed to hear and with which there was heartfelt agreement: "I have never been angry with God for evil. For me there are three symbols: waiting, presence, and silence."

In this discussion, as in all other matters, there was a deep sense of empathy and an awareness of participation in a community. ◀

From the black experience we learn that there are ways of posing the question of God and history, and ways of addressing it, especially from within a community, that avoid the either-or trap: either God is directly responsible for everything by direct action or by neglect, so God causes evil; or God has no part in history at all and is responsible for nothing. The discovery that there is an alternative to the trap is welcome because, while we hesitate to speak about specific mighty acts of God, we do not want to declare that God and history are totally separate. We realize it is very easy when we speak of what God is doing in the world to say more than we should or less than we can, and we understand the challenge: "I have no reason to listen more to those who claim to speak for God than to those who do not make such a claim. God may work in strange ways and places. God may work more in Ford Motor Company than in a particular church group. Certainly I have found people in corporate management as devoted as those in church activities."

THE DIFFICULTIES DO NOT HAVE
THE LAST WORD

It is not easy to discern where God works in history, either in our time or in the past, or to claim just how God works in our midst. It is not easy to give a satisfying answer to those whose confession of God is uncertain even about whether God works in history. The problem of evil, the failures of the churches, the fumbling and unclarity of the human condition do not disappear in the confession of faith. But in that confession, these difficulties do not have the last word.

From the voices of many on the receiving end of much suffering and evil, who have earned the right to say no to the invitation of faith, we hear a different answer—one that says yes to the God to whom the Bible and the Christian tradition point in obedience and in hope. If the existence of evil is an insuperable barrier to confession of faith in God, then that confession cannot exist. But it does exist, and we can hear its voice—and that voice may fairly be allowed to have the last word and to echo in the waiting, the presence, and the silence.

Those who seek to confess faith in God do not have to be busy about asking, "How can God let these things happen?" or even "How can we recognize what God is doing?" They may rather settle for asking, "How can we recognize what is worthy of the God whom we confess?" and "What is given for us to do and to be if we are to be faithful to our confession?"

To the confessor, the world has not been abandoned or neglected. "The intimacy of God's relation to the creation is not in question." But confession recognizes that our responsibility is an inescapable part of what it must mean for God to act in the world. "The question of the Bible is thus not whose side is God on, but what is happening and how do we respond to God's call?" "If we Christians of the world would begin to see God at work in history or even God summoning our work in history, and would—together—put our faith and love into action, that would be a real and unmistakable confession of our faith in God."

PARTNERSHIP

"Christians of the world—together." If so many American Christians have little awareness of the universal church —Christ's family in all six continents—then they will be biased in recognizing what God is doing in our time.

▶ To confess God rightly, we American Christians should listen with a sense of partnership to what Christians outside the U.S. have to say about our nation's role in the world, and should respond as members of the universal body of the church. Otherwise we are in danger of measuring the role of our nation only by our own standards and of considering the universal church as only a spiritual reality, removed from space and time.

Do American Christians listen to others and act as members of the universal church? A few do, but they tend to be isolated from one another. ◀

▶ My concern about nuclear weapons up to now has been largely theoretical. What will make my confessing faith in God in relation to that issue more active? One thing, at least, can help: an attentive listening to the voices of the universal church, particularly in those parts of the world which feel utterly powerless in the face of the superpowers' deadly game of superiority. The instructions from Third World Christians about the confessing we American Christians should be doing to our own nation have not gotten through to me yet. I probably haven't wanted them to. ◀

Listening—that is the clue to learning how to recognize what God is doing in our world. The intervention of God in history is primarily in the speech of God, a speech which most often comes indirectly, but not necessarily indistinctly. "The experiences of God's presence in history are communications events, requiring interpretation." Confession of faith in God requires disciplined listening for the speech of God. Those of us whose voices have been heard the longest, who are most accustomed to speaking, are particularly bad at listening; we are so out of practice.

▶ On both the individual and social levels, God moves in mysterious ways and takes the initiative in paradoxical and unexpected ways. In relation to world history and especially public history, this means that God picks the most unlikely agents—the people Israel, a carpenter's son of the common people, a variety of menials and kooks for prophets, fishermen, the mendicant orders, the "locusts out of the bottom of the pit" (as some of the Radical Puritans were called), the illiterate rabble of Paris, the colonists on the wilderness edge of civilization.

It is usually the marginal, the weak, and the despised who end up in the perspective of salvation history as the central, the powerful, and the revered. Here I gladly call on Scripture as an authority. It is unmistakably clear to me in both the Old and the New Testaments: the cutting edge, the action, although hidden to the establishment at the time, is with the enemies of the establishment.

So I am predisposed to find the movements most clearly related to the coming of the kingdom of God—that is, God provides the lasting dynamics of history by being within those movements—among the marginal, dispossessed, poor, despised. Their spokespersons clearly speak the message of God. Not all movements of the dispossessed are God-inspired; they have to be assessed in light of Scripture, tradition, and conscience. But the God-inspired are among the dispossessed.

Now the relation between the marginal and their

counterparts—the ecclesiastical, political, and cultural establishment (including even the members of the establishment sympathetic to the marginal)—is complex. I don't wish to argue that we of the establishment in America are wholly cut off from the experience of marginalization. But we are the Pharisees, the priestly and Sadducean caste and its lay supporters, the rich of the earth. And the Bible makes clear the chasm between the establishment and the marginals. There is no easy bridge from one to the other. Jesus didn't say to the Pharisees and Sadducees: "Think about your situation and add some new dimensions to your ministry and stewardship," but "You brood of vipers!" He didn't say to the rich: "Think about the opportunities of someone in your position to help," but "It is easier for a camel to go through the eye of a needle . . . ."

The implication is clear: we are not the ones to speak for God's action in history today. By our centrality we are marginalized as spokespersons for God. Maybe it is our job to strive like hell to avoid the hell of the rich man, quietly cling to God's mercy, and let those who are better positioned confess God loudly for the public's benefit. Maybe we have little to confess of interest to anybody. Maybe we should listen, without quibbling, without impulsively defending ourselves. ◀

LISTENING AND SPEAKING

"Maybe we should listen." But our listening should lead to new speech. The relation between what is happening and faith in God is not an abstract question about how well God is managing current history; to ask that question is to take ourselves out of history, to treat faith at arm's length where it becomes an intellectual problem, not a confessional challenge.

▶ If we were to probe the content of our confession to the most basic level, what would we say to each other? Would it not have to concern what causes us greatest despair and, at the same time, where we find cause for hope?

All of us are receiving signals of impending doom for our planet, even if we try to filter the signals out. What is our response? If anxiety leads to psychic numbing as a general condition of nearly all of us, then we cannot move on to any genuine causes for hope on this planet. The threats are too great.

If we will not tell each other what the major faith problem for us is, we will get away with temporizing, rationalizing, or remaining silent. If we will share our images of despair, we may come through to fresh images and possibilities for visioning a future that yet could be.

Our pent-up love for each other, for our earth home, and for those yet to inhabit it (we do not so much inherit the earth from our ancestors as borrow it from our children), will only be released and acted upon as we confess to and with each other concerning the heart of the matter for each of us. ◀

Faith in God does not guarantee that we see everything in proper perspective, but faith in God won't let us evade the issue of evil.

▶ All kinds of evils are jubilating in our time. Can we agree on what the paramount evil is? I would suggest it is the increasingly chilling climate, like an ice age of insult aimed at our humanness, insult we help administer to ourselves, for example, by withdrawing traditional protections from our supremely helpless ones, those who have nothing but life. Insult so demoralizes that we lose vital interest in ourselves and start living by lunges. We live in a time of ever widening permission, even official, to write off certain categories of persons as superfluous, for example, defectives. The new ice age is the age of the superfluous person—an old idea, yes, but now becoming our official way. To Christ, there is no superfluous human, not even one that he isn't prepared to break his neck for. ◀

THE QUESTION TURNS BACK ON US

In the act of confessing faith in God, the question of God and history turns back on me: "If God is indeed in history, then it is through me that God's presence is now embodied." The problem of evil doesn't go away, but it doesn't devour me. I am pressed not to despair, but to repentance. "I may know that I am not monstrous, but I must come to realize that I too am in the grip of 'principalities and powers' beyond my control—the demonic forces of fallen history. My individual sins of omission and my concern for self-fulfillment in apparently innocent ways have contributed to cultural assumptions and institutions that virtually endow evil with a life of its own. I too am dehumanized and powerless."

▶ My faith says that nuclear warfare is a threat; racism, sexism, and other dangers may assail, but ultimately life triumphs. Spiritual death comes when I do not struggle to work on behalf of humanity for justice, equality, and concrete expressions of love. Physical death may come when I do struggle for these things, but that's all right because death is not death! This is so because God has a hand in the struggle and in the outcome. This is what the resurrection says. This is our vision and our hope. ◀

At this point we may acutely sense our personal need

and that of others for the corporate worship of the church. To share in speaking aloud our deep sense of guilt and unworthiness, to hear the age-old words, "Come unto me," to experience however inadequately our kinship with believers of every kind, can give us new strength to continue the search and the struggle.

▶ Communicating with one another is at the core of confessional faith. We try as a confessing community to speak of God from the heart in the circle of our sisters and brothers. So whatever lies in our hearts is prime matter for confession. Be they family troubles, the cheapening of life through abortion, or the threat of nuclear disaster, our ethical concerns should move us to confessional sharing. Be they family joys, beauties seen in prayer, or unexpected gifts, the times when we are surprised by joy also should be shared in Christ's body. Confessing is good for the soul because it is not good for any of us to suffer or rejoice alone. Confessing is good for the church because the church is most itself when we speak forth from the heart our seeking after God and our pursuit of justice. ◀

We listen for the speech of God and, as so often in the experience of the people of God, we hear "a call that both demands and promises transformation and is thus a call of both judgment and grace." That speech, for many of us, becomes clearest in the heart of the gospel message.

▶ Our confession of faith in God must acknowledge that evil and suffering are taken up into the very life of God. For me this means relating God's life to the world's history in and through Jesus Christ and the Holy Spirit, the "giver of life." This is precisely to move toward the future with a more clearly biblical conception of a living God. In other words, a more serious confession of Jesus as a self-disclosure of God will help us avoid the inadequate, even misleading notion of a Supreme Being stepping from time to time into the causal order of history and nature. ◄

▶ I call on Jesus as an authority. Jesus is the center (as John 1 says, "all things were made through him, and without him was not anything made that was made") who becomes margin ("crucified outside the gate," according to Hebrews 13; "emptying himself," according to Philippians 2). From the uttermost position of marginalization, Jesus establishes his authority. Authority and love meet, and reliability is demonstrated. ◄

▶ To confess faith in God means that I (or my race, country, sex, and so forth) and my needs are no longer at the center of my universe or the determiners of my values. God is the center and calls all ethnocentrisms, all chauvinisms, into question. ◄

This living God whom we find at the center can be a comfort, but a strange sort of comfort.

▶ The lives of people past and present have handed on to me more about God than theological speculations: the lesson that peace with God means conflict. The more I accept God, cleansed from my projections of the worst in me and our projections of the worst in us, the more my faith develops into hope and causes unrest and impatience. I have come to be at ease, finally, with the uneasiness of an incarnational faith. ◄

Conclusion: The Beginning

"Now that I am finished, I am beginning." This conclusion of the Introduction was not a boast. It was an admission or, to be more precise, a confession. It ends the Introduction for the same reason that it now begins the Conclusion: it is simply the truth of our experience. As we ended our several summers of conversations, it felt like a beginning.

We fumbled and struggled at first to say who and where we were. We wrestled with ourselves and each other through the years; as we listened and changed, we came slowly to realize that what we share lies deeper than what divides us. What we learned from one another took us further into those sharing depths. As the questions multiplied, the closest we came to a satisfying answer was in what we had not thought in the beginning to ask:

"Does the pilgrimage work?"

"Maybe it will, maybe it won't."

"Tell me how to make the pilgrimage."

"I can't; you have to join the search."

"Well, if that's what it takes, at least show me your goals."

"The goal is a surprise."

The goal will still surprise. The God whom we came together to confess and whom we learned to confess together is a God of surprises. There is no use trying to summarize any further what we came to. We readily admit the limits and partiality of our own confessing and the impossibility of saying everything at once. We are on our way, continuing the search for how best to speak, show, and act the love of God.

Besides, it is not so much why we came that is important, but why we decide to stay. The staying is not in a place, but in a journey, in a work, in a confession.

We end, therefore, in our new beginning, with the voices that sustained and taught and changed us, and that remind us now, as they reminded us then, where we have been and where we are and what our confession now calls us to do. These are the voices of the end and of the beginning. They do not try to be inspiring. They try only to confess—and to invite.